Reflective Practice for Teaching in Lifelong Learning

This book speaks with academic authority and the experience and understanding of practitioners. The authors draw teachers into their world of everyday reflective practice that is much more than a requirement from trainee teachers, but rather is at the heart of all teachers' practice. The authors highlight its value for improving teaching and learning and coping with ongoing change, whilst recognising honestly the difficulties in making time to reflect deeply and critically and the questions raised about the worth of reflective practice in an increasingly regulated sector. Rich examples bring the text to life, exemplify concepts and demonstrate practical applications.

Mary Samuels, Oxford Brookes University, UK.

This book has a heartening and optimistic message at its centre: reflective practice can help us as teachers discover what actually works to improve practice, not what should work or what we've been told might work. It is written in a refreshingly straightforward way that steers clear of educational jargon and aims for clarity; it is an antidote to the over-theorizing of Reflective Practice that it warns against.

Noelle Graal, Canterbury Christ Church University, UK.

The authors of this clear and informative book have delved into their extensive experience to produce a must have text for all those who care about the state of teaching and learning in the Lifelong Learning sector. By providing an in depth, detailed and critical account of the key processes and products of reflective practice their book must become a set text on initial teacher training courses for the sector and an essential resource for both tutors and managers.

Dr Graham Hitchcock, University Centre, Doncaster, UK.

Reflective Practice for Teaching in Lifelong Learning

Ian Rushton and Martin Suter

Mc Graw Hill Open University Press

Open University Press
McGraw-Hill Education
McGraw-Hill House
Shoppenhangers Road
Maidenhead
Berkshire
England
SL6 2QL

email: enquiries@openup.co.uk
world wide web: www.openup.co.uk

and Two Penn Plaza, New York, NY 10121-2289, USA

First published 2012

A catalogue record of this book is available from the British Library

ISBN-13: 978-0-33-524401-0 (pb)
ISBN-10: 0-33-524401-7 (pb)
eISBN: 978-0-33-524402-7

Library of Congress Cataloging-in-Publication Data
CIP data applied for

Typesetting and e-book compilations by
RefineCatch Limited, Bungay, Suffolk
Printed and bound in the UK by Bell & Bain Ltd, Glasgow

The *McGraw-Hill* Companies

Contents

Acronyms and abbreviations

AB	Awarding Body
BTEC	British and Technology Education Council
CPD	continuing professional development
DTLLS	Diploma in Teaching in the Lifelong Learning Sector
EM	external moderator
EV	external verifier
FE	further education
FENTO	Further Education National Training Organisation
HEI	higher education institution
HND	Higher National Diploma
IfL	Institute for Learning
ILP	individual learning plan
ITE	initial teacher education
LLS	lifelong learning sector
NVQ	national vocational qualification
OSAT	On-Site Assessment and Training
PDP	personal development plan
QTLS	Qualified Teacher Learning and Skills
QTS	qualified teacher status
RSA	Royal Society of Arts
SAR	Self Assessment Report
SFA	Skills Funding Agency
SVUK	Standards Verification UK
WBE	work based experience
YPLA	Young People's Learning Agency

1

Why reflect on practice?

We have produced this book with the aim of demystifying reflective practice and taking teacher reflection back to its rightful owner – you. In the same way that the 2010 coalition government partly cleared the national decks by throwing out some quangos and bureaucracy, we have attempted to throw everything out of the reflective practice 'shed' and brought back in only those things that you really need to know and use. In doing so, what we expect you to get out of this book on reflective practice is a refreshing, painless and commonsense view of teaching and learning as it affects you and your groups as well as the confidence to take ownership of how your teaching role can be better managed.

Reflection comes from the latin word *reflectere* (to bend back) and which Hanks (1979: 1227) usefully defines as 'to think, meditate or ponder'. If we are to take this definition as a working hypothesis we can say that reflective practice is concerned with the teacher thinking, meditating or pondering over the day, the last session, the needy student at break-time, the fruitful discussion that came out of the risky newspaper article and the waiting marking pile, etc. In other words, reflective practice is concerned with the everyday practice, challenges and triumphs of the teacher's working day whether the context is a further education (FE) college, university, prison, sixth form, hospital ward, fire station practice yard or any of the dozens of other places where those aged 14 years or above learn, develop and hone their skills, knowledge and understanding. Despite the diversity of the lifelong learning sector (LLS), here we are at the crux of what teachers throughout the sector share in common – the everyday practice of teaching and learning which Furlong (2003: 18) describes as: 'Rather than inhabiting the "high ground" of professional certainty, they [teaching professionals] have to work in the "swampy lowlands" of everyday life, facing situations that are complicated and messy, defying easy technical solutions'.

Yet reflecting on our teaching, and the ways in which our students learn from what we do in our taught sessions, is a contingent practice and depends on the conditions and context at the time. For example, assessing students' achievements of the learning outcomes for a session relies on completely different techniques for an A-level business studies session than it would for trainee firefighters practising the pump drill. Likewise, reflecting on an introductory arts and crafts session in an all-female prison will identify different issues and areas for improvement than the last time the same course was commenced in the same institution because there are different learners involved.

For trainee teachers, reflective practice has enjoyed a privileged position in initial teacher education (ITE) since the mid-1990s where many authors have sought to advance a set of effective approaches which lead trainee teachers from their first unsteady steps to a life of autonomy – confident and independent in front of class. Yet libraries and staffrooms throughout the LLS are awash with books, journals, training event packs and opportunities for further continuing professional development (CPD) that work, re-work and re-work again reflective practice in the apparent pursuit of a holy grail of reflective practice that can be taken as a cure-all for improving all teaching and learning. In 1995 Maynard and Furlong (p. 16) summed up this apparent frenzy well as 'Trainees today are constantly urged to reflect, though it is not always made explicit what reflection means or what they should be reflecting on'. Yet ten years after Maynard and Furlong, Jarvis (2005) suggested that little had changed where, 'The term [reflection] has become so widely and inconsistently used that it has to some extent been devalued' (Jarvis 2005: 8). Given that little has changed since the mid-2000s aside from some tightening of the regulations, there is little wonder that reflective practice has begun to attract criticism in some quarters.

We echo these sentiments and suggest that over-theorized reflective practice has been seen to move us back from what teachers recognize as ordinary and everyday to a place where multiple models and frameworks of reflective practice serve only to confuse and demotivate many trainees. Here, reflective practice has become shrouded in a discourse of regulation, accreditation, professional standards and even surveillance, which we intend to clear up. While there is a literature that promotes reflective practice as an integral component of what the trainee teacher is expected to do – and the two preceding quotes allude to some of this – it suggests that trainee teachers labour under what is perceived to be reflective practice as a burden, a necessary evil that will be caged once a full teaching qualification is achieved. In this book, therefore, we will be advancing a commonsense framework of reflective practice which seeks to cater for all three categories while accommodating the Professional Standards (LLUK 2005).

In contrast, the experienced teacher can be lulled into a position where teaching and learning are seen as mundane and ordinary with little scope to make them otherwise and we also have such teachers in mind as we write this book and argue that experienced teachers reflect in similar, if not the same, ways to trainees although it becomes somehow 'easier' and less of a burden. The reasons for this are that, put simply, the more experience a teacher has the more resources there are in the cupboard, resources that are comprised of knowledge, techniques and ideas. An example might be where an experienced teacher has a new group of national vocational qualification (NVQ) level 2 learners arrive at their own list of ground rules on their first day because they are most likely to suggest sensible and 'acceptable' rules like, 'Turn off mobile phones; respect others' opinions', etc. By the third session the teacher may have cause to ask them, 'Remind me of *your* ground rules regarding mobile phones', an often effective strategy for addressing a common distraction during a session. Given that the trainee teacher is unlikely to have been given such a group on their first day, yet experienced the mobile phone problem later, they might have to work hard to arrive at the idea which can be piloted when they get a new group, although the experienced teacher automatically uses it with every new group because of its success in the past on many occasions. Thus, experienced teachers often manage their practice and their classes with a degree of apparent fluency and ease, yet they are not always aware when and why some things do not work and this book, therefore, is intended for them also.

There are many reasons for reflecting on practice and it is useful for our purposes here to group them into three categories:

- improving and developing teaching and learning;
- accommodating change;
- complying with regulatory systems.

Such groupings offer the notion that reflective practice is not preserved solely for the teacher, either trainee or experienced, but that all involved in the provision, support, development and evaluation of teaching and learning in the LLS can and should use reflective practice as a core function of their role. While there is considerable overlap between the three categories, and arguing that all are essential in their own ways, we suggest that there is a notable inequality in the importance of each which can be portrayed as a Venn diagram (see Figure 1.1).

We are aware that such an approximation of the inequalities sits uneasily with the way reflective practice has been felt to impact on teachers in the sector over recent

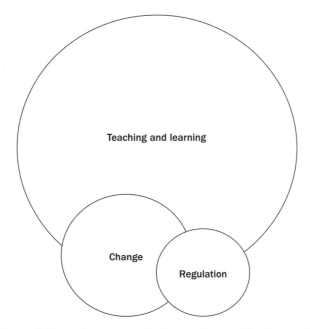

Figure 1.1 Thematic reasons for the teacher to reflect on practice

years, for example the twin forces of constant change and the performative burden in the sector, yet such a framework is the basic premise of this book. We further suggest that the small space where the three circles overlap represents the context in which each of us operates: a context comprised of subject specialism, institution, learning site(s), certain education policies and the local cultural and social debates that filter down into our swampy lowlands.

Taking the three categories or circles as thematic reasons for reflecting on our practice, we can start to explore the finer reasons behind each in the following order:

- improving and developing teaching and learning;
- coping with change in the job role and/or organization;
- complying with regulatory systems.

Improving and developing teaching and learning

First, the development of teaching and learning is central to what we do in the sector although the notion of improvement of either or both is a potential minefield and assumes, as do Ofsted, that there is a need for continual improvement. Without being drawn into that argument for the moment, let us say then that teaching and learning can be developed, and often improved, as a result of *pondering, thinking and meditating* on experience. Another point of tension is that, as an LLS practitioner, you may be wary of numerous competing definitions of what constitutes 'effective teaching' or 'effective learning' ranging from your colleagues' ideas of what is required in classes, through the organization's notions or benchmarks of effective teaching and behaviours to Ofsted's perceived tick box approach.

Given the unique and contingent nature of your teaching role and context, we suggest that you arrive at your own definition of what constitutes good or effective teaching and learning before reading further. Yet this is no easy option since it should carefully draw together what you believe is educationally desirable in your context and specialism, a set of professional values that you adhere to firmly and which you can defend with good reason. To adopt someone else's definition could lumber you with a set of core values that might be inauthentic for you and, if you intend to be true to yourself and your learners, you need to grow your own identity as a unique feature of your sense of professionalism.

For example, a plumbing lecturer may hold fast to the belief that their primary role is to carefully mould the next generation of skilled plumbers, a personal core value that is seen in their taught sessions by frequently locating the learning alongside their anecdotal evidence and the developing workplace experience of the apprentice plumbers. Or a Higher National Diploma (HND) engineering tutor may be a true believer in the value of developing learners' independent thinking and reasoning characterized by regular workplace investigations and directed individual study. Alternatively, a basic skills tutor in a Young Offender Institution may have chosen to work in that setting through adherence to a belief that everyone deserves a second chance, an outplaying of social justice and humanism which surfaces in each session as encouragement, motivation and unconditional positive regard. In contrast, if your core value is to convert enrolments into certificates by the end of the year, come what may, you may struggle with the tenor of this book.

Improving and developing teaching

None of us is the finished product and, given that we should be looking to change learning activities before our learners' attention spans expire (on average, approximately one minute per year of age up to a maximum of 20 minutes), we need to develop a range of available teaching and learning techniques that provide variety and stimulation. As we think around new ideas or teaching and learning strategies, we are also mindful that they should suit the students' needs, learning styles and preferences – not the other way round. Here, the smart thinking works hard to simultaneously improve other aspects of teaching, for example, identifying a change of focus that also assesses learning from the last activity thereby providing variety in assessment (Domain B of the LLUK standards acts as a useful set of prompts here). Teachers, especially trainees when their teaching practice is being observed, have a tendency to rely on activities that are reinforced by the various theories of learning. While such an approach is both recommended and reliable, we offer two additional touchstones from which teaching practice can possibly be developed in a non-threatening way: first, when each of us stood before our first class we probably had no theories to rely on but drew on our experiences as learners to guide our first session – this is a useful datum that we should not lose sight of because, at that time, we had to think like learners and should continue to do so; second, the way that theories sit with practice vary from one group to another, one subject specialism to another and so on – this is one way of thinking about praxis or context where the three categories in the Venn diagram come together and which Wilson (1994: 201) summarizes well:

> Praxis is reflecting on what we do, the ends to which action is intended, the means by which it is achieved, the context in which it occurs, the standards by which it is judged, and finally, most importantly, the essential rightness or wrongness of our practice as adult educators.

Thus, we suggest that any improvement or development of teaching should concentrate on what can and should occur in our contexts while being pragmatic about what we can use. Here, we are mindful of resource and cost limitations, the availability of rooms and up to date artefacts, the appropriateness of visiting speakers as a cost-effective alternative to an industrial visit, etc. As subject specialists in our institutions, we know what is available, possible and achievable so we work with what we have in order to improve and develop our teaching practice. As we exploit the resources and facilities available to us in new and innovative ways, we should expect some disasters where the learners did not take to a particular resource, failed to make the link between their own workplace experience and the newspaper court report or did not contribute equally in small groups to produce a poster, etc. as we thought they would. This is good and normal and even Ofsted encourage trainees to take risks – providing they learn from them.

Improving and developing learning

The fundamental reasons for improving and developing learning are to enhance the learners' experience (if you are a learner-centred teacher) and to achieve the learning outcomes of the session, module or award (if you are more teacher-centred). In an ideal world you will strive to achieve both while making the learning process as developmental and enjoyable as possible for both yourself and your learners.

As we have seen already, reflective practice is concerned with *thinking, meditating or pondering* over the learning process and one of the best sources of material for reflection is to ask the students. It is one thing to recognize that the peer assessment activity worked well to bring together the learners into meaningful dialogue where their opinions were clearly heard and justified, and quite another to appreciate why it worked well from their perspective. Until we ask, we are simply second-guessing and nowhere nearer to answering the fundamental questions of whether the learning met their personal needs, why it worked for them and how we can build on such small successes.

Coping with change in the job role and/or organization

Given the diverse nature of our learners and the sector, reflective practice and professional development needs to be an ongoing, constructive spiral of professional development, learning and growth that never stops. We suggest that there are three reasons why accommodating change should inform some of our reflective practice given that such change is often imposed.

Because your organization can change

The last Labour government gained a heard-earned reputation for setting out revised education initiatives in the post-14 sector with a string of education ministers (even if they did not consider education to be sufficiently important to include it in the ministerial title) seeking to leave their legacy before swiftly moving to a new department. Such momentum, or 'policy hysteria' (Keep 2006: 59), tends to shape the identities of both teaching organizations and professionals by a particular demand-driven language and thinking which effectively channels those affected into compliance. For example, the Foster review (2005) of FE colleges and the Leitch review (2006) of skills acknowledged the central importance of the sector but advocated the need for radical reforms of how the sector is set up and managed both locally and nationally. In their wake, and as an example of ensuing change, *Further Education Colleges – Models for Success* (DIUS 2008) amounted to a set of 'to boldly go' imperatives where training organizations were encouraged to merge, streamline and cater for the assessment needs of industry through a change culture epitomized as follows: 'Customer-centred delivery models will require colleges to reassess what they are doing and how. ... It may require different approaches to managing the college workforce' (DIUS 2008: 10). At the time of writing, while we await the outcomes of the Wolf review (the old chestnut of trying to suggest a vocational learning alternative for 14–19-year-olds), we see the coalition government's twin emphasis of skills reform and funding reform lurking in the doorway. Hence, training organizations throughout the sector remain in a seemingly constant state of change.

The only reliable constant in all of this is that, regardless of whatever reforms or initiatives are being brewed or hatched, the post-14 sector needs good teachers. Whatever new thing is next to land on our desks, employers, students, governments and industry stakeholders need our teaching skills. So be encouraged at this time of flux – this book will give you, the subject specialist and teaching professional, the reflective skills and confidence to absorb change, develop the required additional skills and to grow in a professional way as your organization and work role change around you.

Because your work role can change

If you are a trainee teacher on a full-time programme you will have noticed the significant differences that a teaching role has made to your life. Even the firefighter who has moved into a training role on the same watch they have worked on for years will have seen the changes to their daily routine. Yet within an established teaching role there are times of change, if not perpetual change, when we wish for the world to stand still, if only for a moment. While such periods of change can seem to swing from minor tinkering to dramatic upheaval, they represent opportunities for personal and professional growth that should not be ignored or avoided.

Reflective practice is probably the most valuable tool in your box of resources and enables you to think both backwards and forwards. This is not to linger over the way things in your job role were, but to learn from the experience, salvage what you need and move forward. Similarly, at every new twist and turn to the job role you should ask yourself, 'Haven't I seen this before? Has my mentor seen this before?'. For example, some practitioners interpreted the introduction of Functional Skills as Key Skills by another name which they, in turn, saw as revamped Core Skills while others viewed the introduction of Foundation degrees as re-badged Higher National Diplomas. There are only so many new things but multiple ways of dressing them so, as your role and responsibilities change, look at what you already have and do then, thinking forward, visualize the ways things could be in the light of experience and resources.

Because you can change

The current political trend of lecturers, tutors and trainers et al. (we are all teachers according to the Professional Standards) becoming the assessment servants of choice seekers from local industry suggests a disregard for teacher autonomy which resonates with Brown et al.'s (2008) notion of educational Taylorism where 'permission to think' (p. 11) is, in the post-14 context, reserved for managers. Very well, but note that you have already been making personal and professional judgements in your working life, decisions that were made in moral and ethical terms and you are well placed to continue making them. Whether a trainee or an experienced teacher, you were chosen for your teaching role, particularly for your subject specialist knowledge and experience, and your biography is yours as you seek to develop it.

We are all on a trajectory of self-improvement and the process of being challenged by changing job roles and shifting institutional structures can be taken as a set of ideas that are both liberating and emancipatory as you take your opportunities to make your voice heard as Pollard (2002: 15) suggests: 'Indeed, it is important that, within a modern democratic society, teachers should be entitled to not only a hearing, but also some influence, on educational policy.' More of this later.

Complying with regulatory systems

Legislative requirements

In addition to the change culture that is firmly embedded in the LLS, another legacy of political interference in the sector is the spectre of regulation that hangs over all teachers and their institutions. The regulations that impact on teachers appear to be devised by either policymakers (who we suggest seem to know little of teaching or learning) or professional bodies who, in all good faith, act as semi-official agents of governmental power to ensure performativity and standardization of teaching and learning across the sector. We could say much on this matter but others have said it well enough as Ball (2003: 215) suggests:

> Performativity, it is argued, is a new mode of state regulation which makes it possible to govern in an 'advanced liberal' way. It requires individual practitioners to organise themselves as a response to targets, indicators and evaluations. To set aside personal beliefs and commitments and live an existence of calculation. The new performative worker is a promiscuous self, an enterprising self, with a passion for excellence.

Commentators may also suggest that the policymakers and power brokers who pick over our teaching practice are content to have us cowering because we invariably become compliant. Yet regulation requires nothing more than what we are already doing. Put simply, here are the fearsome players who impact on the teaching role and what they require:

Ofsted
This is a quango who make judgements about your institution based on statistical data. In other words, they probably know the grade that they will award before they arrive at your college every four years and, in the unlikely event that they observe one of your sessions, nothing you can do at the front of class will improve that grade, so relax. Ofsted were also responsible for having the government require all new teachers to the sector (from 2007 and any longer-serving teachers who change organizations after 2007) to acquire a teaching qualification appropriate to their job role. Ofsted monitor the quality of this provision, including your mentor arrangements, through inspecting the ITE programme on which you are a student teacher. Again, in the unlikely event that on Ofsted inspector comes to observe one of your sessions, they will use a watered-down version of the inspection criteria and make allowances for you being a trainee.

LLUK

This is another quango and the one that wrote the professional standards that underpin our teaching practice although, at the time of writing, LLUK have been told by the government that their funding will cease. Standards Verification UK (SVUK) is an LLUK subsidiary and their inspections of ITE programmes should also fall by the wayside quite soon although the Professional Standards are likely to be with us for several years and have a direct relationship with reflective practice throughout this book.

Further Education National Training Organisation (FENTO)

This organization wrote the earlier professional standards for teachers which were revised by LLUK because they were inappropriate for trainee teachers. Ignore any of this if you come across it.

Institute for Learning (IfL)

This is a professional body, much like other professional institutes who represent the views of their membership in industry and elsewhere in the workplace, who represent teachers in the LLS in much the same way that the General Teaching Council (GTC and recently deceased) represented school teachers. The IfL are currently fighting on a number of fronts, for example lobbying government for funding and giving teachers in the sector a voice etc., but they also manage our continuing professional development (CPD) records as we will see in Chapter 7. Any teacher in the LLS pursuing the status of QTLS (Qualified Teacher Learning and Skills), an almost-equivalent of qualified teacher status (QTS) for school teachers (but unlikely ever to achieve parity because someone would then need to pay us the same), would need to work with the IfL over the year following completion of their full teaching qualification (a year of 'Professional Formation' culminating in QTLS status). The IfL, like other professional institutes, also have a disciplinary role where members are brought to account for allegedly bringing the profession into disrepute (therefore, avoid risky websites, inappropriate relations with your students, fights and anything you would not want your mother to know about).

Awarding Bodies (ABs)

These are the bodies who issue certificates to your successful students, for example City & Guilds, Edexcel, RSA and Open College, etc. and who monitor your programme through annual visits by an external verifier (EV) or external moderator (EM). Current crises in funding mean that some of this is now conducted through the post but you may receive an annual visit and an observation of your teaching. EVs and EMs tend to be highly experienced, pragmatic and supportive professionals who wish to leave you better than they found you by sharing some of the good practice they have seen elsewhere. What they will want to see from you as a teacher on their programme include:

- course file (a working document or everything you use on the programme. Your programme leader has a centre handbook that lists everything that should be in there);

- up to date CV (you will already have this);
- CPD record for the last year (see Chapter 7);
- CPD plan for the coming six months (again, see Chapter 7).

If you are a trainee teacher on a Diploma in Teaching in the Lifelong Learning Sector (DTLLS) type programme and your teaching is observed during an annual visit, the programme leader and tutors of your ITE programme would bear the full force of anything in your teaching practice that the EV/EM wished to challenge. Where you teach on a higher education institute's (HEI) network of programmes, for example a degree course delivered in a local FE college, your organization enjoys a periodic revalidation similar to an Awarding Body visit, but it is likely to be every three or four years. Again, course file, CVs and CPD records will be required.

Your own institution
One of the ways in which the quality of teaching and learning, and by implication the quality of the programmes on which you teach in your job role, is assessed is through self assessment by the organization you work for. The depth and rigour of such systems vary throughout the sector and you should consult your organization's Quality Assurance Manual or Handbook for what is required of you (see also Chapter 4). While any internal system requires you to maintain the sort of records that the ABs require, one of the most common systems is for two of your taught sessions to be observed each year by either an experienced professional (e.g. an Advanced Practitioner) or a member of the managerial team in the organization. You should receive at least two weeks prior notice of an observation and clear criteria for the ensuing grade that is identical to the Ofsted criteria. There should also be an opportunity for you to discuss and challenge the observer's comments, with a right of appeal if you disagree with the grade, and the final grade remains confidential between you, the observer and your curriculum manager who will throw your grades into the mix when you have your annual appraisal or review.

To demonstrate professional values in accordance with standards
The LLUK professional standards can be said to have three strands:

- Domain A: an overarching professional ethos that underpins the other five domains.
- Domains B–F: each of these sections (learning and teaching; specialist learning and teaching; planning for learning; assessment for learning; and access and progression, respectively) has two strands – professional knowledge and understanding and professional practice.

Demonstrating that we teach according to the professional standards, therefore, might be evidenced from two key sources. First, professional practice will be seen in your session plans, course file, feedback on any observed sessions and the data for your annual appraisal or review while any additional evidence would be a bonus. Second, your professional knowledge and understanding is foremost in your teaching qualification (when achieved) and course files and various sources of feedback while still training. Ongoing evidence of continually developing knowledge and understanding should be a feature of your CPD record and planned future CPD. Given that there are no surprises in the Professional Standards and nothing that you would not know, understand or be doing, then they should hold no fear for you.

We suggest, therefore, that your CPD and any evidence of reflective practice be primary sources of evidence should anyone ask for them. Since we will explore CPD in Chapter 7 it will suffice here to say that your reflective practice is a priceless tool on your way to qualification and can inform your teaching qualification written work as it does your teaching practice.

Here, you are at will to challenge the flawed notions that learning can be packaged; the policymakers' assumptions about one-size-fits-all teaching and learning; Ofsted's methodology that ticking all the boxes represents outstanding teaching; the government's perceived deficit model of teaching; and that measurements of effective teaching and learning can be judged objectively.

In contrast, you may argue that teaching is an art, not a science, and when it is judged to be of high quality that is a value judgement rather than an exercise in box-ticking; that, despite intensification of work roles and preparation time being eroded, you see great things happening around you each day; that despite conditions in the sector being well below optimum for high quality teaching and learning you see colleagues and learners making great strides with what they have.

Therefore, be pragmatic and let your core values and principles (possibly the reason you decided to be a teacher in the sector in the first place) guide you to do the best you can with what you have available at the time. In other words, be both idealistic yet realistic and be encouraged by Thompson and William (2007) who found that teacher quality is one of the greatest influences on learner achievement and attainment.

Useful links

Lifelong Learning UK: www.lluk.org.uk
Institute for Learning: www.ifl.ac.uk
OurSubject (professional teacher network): http://oursubject.hud.ac.uk

2

A basic model of reflective practice

In our experience, there are often two aspects of reflective practice which give the student teacher cause for concern: actually getting started on the process of reflection and reflective writing. This chapter will draw upon realistic scenarios in teaching and learning to illustrate how to get started. First the basic process of reflection will be outlined using a basic model of reflection (see Figure 2.1) that can be used right away to consider aspects of a teacher's professional practice in the classroom and workshop. Second, there will be a consideration of the development of reflective writing skills.

Practice

The process starts with the professional practice of the teacher. In this chapter we will consider that to be the teaching and learning for which the individual teacher is

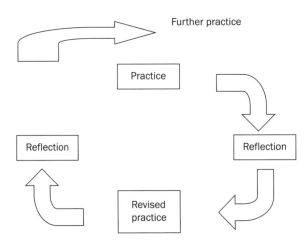

Figure 2.1 A basic model of reflection
Source: Reynolds and Suter (2010)

responsible in the classroom or workshop. Professional practice of course encompasses more than this, and the wider aspects will be considered in later chapters. The next stage is the reflection on what has gone on in the teaching and learning situation. This reflection might be an evaluation of teaching and learning, a consideration for example of whether the stated learning outcomes set for a session have been achieved, and if not why not. Reflection may however be prompted by a particular issue in the teaching and learning situation which needs to be resolved, perhaps problems with classroom management. At this stage the teacher will give consideration to how aspects of teaching and learning might be improved, or problems resolved. These reflections result in a revised practice, where the teacher makes the changes necessary to change and make improvements to teaching and learning. This is followed by another stage of reflection where the teacher will ask whether the changes they made to their professional practice had the desired effect.

Let us now consider each of the stages in more detail, drawing on examples from across the LLS. We start with the teaching and learning situation.

Pamela is a student teacher on a full-time Certificate in Education course and has a placement in the local further education college. As part of her teaching practice she has been teaching psychology on a part-time Level 3 child care course. Syed is also on a full time Certificate in Education course. His placement is in adult education teaching numeracy, mainly at Level 2. Julie teaches for a voluntary organization which works with young people who for a variety of reasons have been unable to take up learning or work opportunities since leaving school. She is on a part-time teacher education course. Alan teaches motor vehicle engineering at a variety of levels in a further education college, with both young people and adults and he has recently completed his teacher training. Each of these professional situations throws up challenges and problems on which the student teachers will need to reflect if they are to be met and resolved.

Pamela has found her engagement with the child care students to be a difficult one. There seems a reluctance in the group to read the materials that she has directed the students to, and even more to discuss theories of psychology in the class. She has asked the group to hand in drafts of assignment work, and Pamela is concerned that most of the students have merely described the theories, with little effort made to relate those theories to actual child care situations. Her mentor at the placement has informed Pamela that the students have approached their course tutor stating that they had difficulty 'understanding' the subject.

Syed feels he has made a positive start to his placement. He is teaching in a variety of adult education centres across the town with students who have often made some progress with their numeracy skills, though he is expected at some centres to teach students of widely different ability. It is one of these groups that is providing Syed with the most challenge. It is a group of 12 adults, eight of whom are working towards a level two award, with the rest working towards Level 1. To accommodate both levels, Syed starts with the Level 1 students, asking the rest to complete a task, and when he has started off the Level 1 students with a task, he spends some time with the Level 2 students as a group. Syed feels this is the best arrangement, and indeed when he was observing his mentor teach, it was an arrangement that worked very well. However there are problems with students interrupting him when he is working with others, either as a group or individually. This is causing considerable problems; Syed is finding it difficult to concentrate and it is consuming precious session time.

Julie's work with young people involves developing their skills and knowledge so they are ready to take advantage of education, training and work opportunities. They come to Julie for a 12-week course, during which time they work on developing interpersonal, organizational, literacy, numeracy and computer skills.

As part of the course the young people work in groups of four or five to organize a small scale fund raising event for a number of local charities. Julie feels that on the whole this activity has worked well, with the trainees using a range of skills and know-ledge learned on the course. She does however feel there are improvements to be made. Julie has noted that some trainees in the groups are often doing more than their fair share of the organizing, with others becoming involved only after a great deal of prompting from the tutor. She has found also that trainees' absence from the course causes problems. Often these absences are unavoidable; the trainees sometimes need to attend interviews, for example. However it does mean that organizing sessions are missed, causing delays and frustration in the other group members.

Alan teaches most of his timetable in a motor vehicle workshop. On the whole he finds the groups of students he teaches there are engaged with the learning; they concentrate during the demonstrations of the various aspects of motor vehicle engi-neering and perform the tasks he sets them with little prompting. There is one element of the workshop sessions that does cause Alan some concern and that is health and safety. Alan and his colleagues feel they pay due regard to health and safety issues in the health and safety workshop. As part of the induction of the students onto the courses, they are given a session on health and safety, with a DVD shown of the risks and hazards in a workshop. Students are required to wear the appropriate personal protective clothing and equipment at all times in the workshop, and this is closely monitored by Alan and his colleagues. Alan notes however that the health and safety awareness of his students does tend to wane. They certainly continue to dress in the appropriate clothing and equipment with little fuss, and there tend to be few prob-lems with 'horse-play' in the workshop. However, some risks begin to get ignored and hazards created. As he walks around the workshop, Alan notes that oil spills have not been dealt with, and cables are left trailing across the floor. Tools are often not put back in place after use and left on surfaces where they may catch a person walking past. Every few sessions with a group of students, Alan has what he calls a 'safety blitz', issuing reminders to the group and individual students about risks and hazards and their responsibilities in the workshop. This approach works for a little while, but then the problems start to re-emerge. Alan wonders if there is another way to tackle the issue.

Reflection

All four teachers are engaged in professional practices which throw up challenges to be faced and problems to be solved. To deal with them will mean giving careful consid-eration to the causes and to possible changes to meet the challenges and solve the problems; this is the 'reflection' stage of the cycle. Perhaps the most straightforward way to start reflecting is for our four teachers to ask themselves a series of questions. The first question is 'what?' – what is the nature of the challenge or issue to be dealt with? A clear answer to this question is important, because it helps us to 'frame' the issue, to 'isolate' it as far as is possible from what else is going on. 'When?' is the next question – is when a challenge or issue occurs a crucial factor? Many teachers find that the concentration levels of learners tend to dip on a Friday afternoon! The third question is 'where?' – the place where teaching and learning takes place may be a factor. Vocational tutors may find that there are more behavioural issues in a theory session than in a practical one. 'Who is involved?' is an important question. Does the issue arise with a whole group of learners, or part of the group or an individual? The last two questions point towards possible responses to challenges and solutions to problems. When the teacher asks the question, 'Why?' they are looking for the reasons for the challenges that occur in teaching and learning. The final question is, 'How?' – how are the challenges to be met and problems solved? Asking this question helps to formulate a plan for implementation which is the next stage of the cycle.

Our four teachers start the process by asking themselves what the issue is. The issue for Pamela is that the students are having difficulty engaging with theories of psychology. For Syed it is that constant interruptions from individual students mean that he is not able to give his full attention other learners. Julie considers the issue to be one of group management; some trainees are not participating fully in project work. For Alan it is health and safety issues – that the awareness of risks and hazards in the workshop wanes over time.

The question 'when' can be used in different ways. Teachers might consider the time of the day a factor, or when during a sequence of learning or of course when in the students' learning careers. Having asked the latter question Pamela is able to ascertain from her mentor that students do not on the whole have difficulty in engaging with theory in other modules on the course. Giving some consideration to the stage of the students' learning careers, Pamela acknowledges that some of the theories she was introducing them to might seem difficult. For Syed, the question 'when?' is a particularly crucial one. The times when the interruptions occur are just when he needs to concentrate on the learning needs of individual or groups of students in the class. It is the timing of these interruptions that makes finding a solution urgent. The question 'when?' for Julie relates to the periodic absence of trainees during the project work. She does acknowledge that an individual might have to absent her/himself for a legitimate reason, but nevertheless these absences do disrupt planning and implementation of the project. However Julie is able to comfort herself that these absences do not only occur during the time of week devoted to the project work. Having reflected upon the question 'when?' Alan concludes that time is an important factor in the issue that faces him in the motor vehicle workshop. It is that over time that the effect of his safety 'blitz' seems to fade and that some aspects of safe working practices are ignored. Alan notes that for a short time after his blitz students do demonstrate an awareness of risks and hazards in the workshop, and there is at least a willingness to work safely. For all our teachers then the question 'when' is an important one, and the asking of it will help to formulate resolution of the issues facing them.

The question of who is involved at first sight is a simple one for our teachers – the answer is the learners they work with. It is however a question that demands closer consideration. Is the challenge or issue one which involves all the learners in a group, or is it part of the group or some individuals? In Pamela's case she is able to ascertain that it is the majority of the group who are having difficulty engaging with psychological theories. When Syed asks himself the question, he reflects that it is the students with lower attainment in the class that tend to interrupt him the most. Furthermore Syed is able to identify the individual students who are most likely to interrupt him on a regular basis. 'Who?' is a more complicated question for Julie. As there is no pattern to the trainee absences, it could be said to be an issue that potentially involves a whole group, or in the rare instances when there are no absences during the project work sessions, involves no one at all. The answer to the question 'who?' where the issue of participation in group work is concerned was more straightforward. Through the monitoring of group activities Julie is able to identify those individuals who are doing more or less of their share. When asking himself the question, Alan was not able to identify any individuals who were more or less likely to ignore risks and hazards. He concludes that health and safety is an issue that will have to be tackled with whole groups of students.

There is another element to the question 'who' that our teachers need to explore: there may be other people in the situation who may need to be considered. In Pamela's case she needs to consider the views of her mentor. This is the person with the responsibility of overseeing Pamela's placement, advising and supporting her. In both the clear identification of issues and resolving them Pamela will need to consult her mentor. Pamela will of course also be able to approach her teacher education tutor for advice and support, probably through a tutorial. Syed is also on a full-time teacher education course and therefore will need to take the views of his placement mentor into account. As with Pamela, Syed has access to his teacher education tutor. Both Julie and Alan may have to take into account the views and actions of colleagues. Have Julie's co-tutors experienced the same issues in small group work, for example?

Alan will have to ascertain from his colleagues how they tackle health and safety issues in the workshop. In both cases it is probable that any resolution of the issues will involve to some extent the agreement and participation of their colleagues. It may be that the resolution of the issues will have to involve their manager. In Julie's case, if changes to the course structure were called for they would of course have to be agreed with the manager of the provision. If there were to be any changes to the layout of the workshop Alan would need to consult with and receive the consent of his manager.

The next question our teachers will ask themselves is 'why' – why are these issues arising in the learning environment? Finding reasons is a crucial step in resolving the issues. Seeking out answers to this question will look back over the responses to the questions above, and will look forward to asking 'how' issues are to be resolved.

Pamela felt she identified what the issue was – that her students had difficulty engaging with theory. However she was puzzled that those same students were evidently understanding theory in other modules on the course, and were in those subjects able to link theory to practice in the workplace, something they seemed unable to do with psychology. With the help of her mentor Pamela investigated the ways other teachers on the course taught theory, and how links were made between theory and practice. It became apparent to Pamela that they used many more examples from the students' work place than she had been doing. Looking back over the comments made by her mentor after an observation of her teaching, Pamela found one which stated that some of her delivery of the theory was 'rather abstract'. This view of her teaching was confirmed a short while later when she was observed by her tutor. She remarked that Pamela was not putting theory 'in context' nearly enough. Pamela reflected that perhaps she had been looking the wrong way, and concerning herself with a 'lack of application' from the learners rather than her own approach to teaching the subject.

Syed felt that he identified what the issue in the classroom was, but what was not clear at this stage was why? Was it a matter of student confidence (or lack of it), was it because he had not established ground rules governing behaviour in the classroom? Like Pamela, Syed approached his placement mentor, who agreed to undertake an observation to specifically look at the issues that concerned Syed. The mentor concurred that there was probably an issue with rules about turn taking, but also that not sufficient time had been spent with the students who had lower attainment. Syed decided that he would have to think again about both the planning and management of the sessions with his students.

Julie was seeking answers to the question 'why' on two issues in her project work with young people. Why were some trainees doing less than their fair share of the tasks in their group? And why were the absences causing such disruption? Julie consulted her colleagues who also used small group work in their sessions. The consensus was that there were three main reasons why individual trainees did not participate fully in group work. First they may not fully understand what is expected of them; second they may not see the relevance of that work to their own development needs; and third there might be an interpersonal issue in that group which may make an individual reluctant to participate. Julie felt that she had already found the reason for the occurrence of the second issue: a trainee was absent, they were not able to undertake a task, therefore there was delay, obviously. However she began to think about the issue from a different perspective: what if the issue was one of the structure of the project work? Perhaps stretching the planning for the charity event over twelve weeks was exacerbating the problems caused by trainee absences. After all, it was inevitable that over that time a significant minority of the trainees would have to take a morning or afternoon off for some reason.

Alan's reflections led him to conjecture that the elapse of time between his safety blitzes was probably a major factor in the motor vehicle workshop. He noted that the lapses in safe working practices increased the further it was since the last session he had addressed health and safety issues. Alan reasoned that he had to find a way of maintaining health and safety awareness over the period of a course and that occasional safety blitzes were not the way to do this.

The last question our teachers will ask themselves is 'how', how will I bring about change in the learning environment that will meet the challenge or resolve the issue? Finding the answer to this question will complete this stage of the reflective cycle and will look forward to the next stage, 'revised practice'. The decisions made on what changes to make will be based on the answers arrived at to all the other questions the teacher has asked him/herself.

Pamela has concluded in her reflections that the issue with her group of learners is less an issue of their lack of ability and more one of her approach to the teaching of psychology. She reasons that if the students do not have the same problems in other classes in engaging with psychology then there might be something to be learned from experienced tutors' approaches that she could develop in her own teaching. Pamela resolves to make stronger links between the various theories, for instance on cognitive development, and what the students experience with children in the nurseries where they work. Consulting her placement mentor once more she makes the necessary changes to the teaching and learning methods and the teaching and learning materials to make these links.

Reflecting on the feedback he has received from his placement mentor, Syed decides he will have to make some changes to the planning of his sessions to take more account of the needs of the learners who have lower attainment. It will be difficult because of the limited time he has, but he takes the decision to spend ten minutes more with the lower level learners in an attempt to ensure they understand what is required of them so that they may work independently. Syed does not feel that this is the whole answer to the problem though. He resolves to visit again the ground rules for this group, emphasizing the need for learners to take their turn in requesting help from the tutor and not interrupting when the tutor is speaking to other learners.

Julie has been facing two related issues with her group of trainees, both concerning small group work. She comes to the conclusion that both the problem of individual engagement (or lack of it) in group activities and that of trainee absence during project work are group management issues. Could the course be structured in such a way as to minimize the disruption caused by absences, and group work managed to ensure the full participation of all the trainees? Julie decides that instead of spreading the project work over the length of the course, she will concentrate it at the end, as a 'grand finale' to the training. She also decides that she will need to be more structuring in the management of the small groups, for instance allotting roles to individual trainees.

Alan has concluded that his strategy of periodic safety blitzes is not working and that he needs to find a better way of raising and maintaining health and safety awareness in the motor vehicle workshop. He reasons that if this awareness fades over time, he must include issues of health and safety in every session with the students. He decides to integrate it into his session planning for all the learning in the workshop.

Revised practice

The next stage of the reflective cycle is where the changes to practice proposed by the teacher are implemented. To ensure that the efficacy of the changes can be properly evaluated (the next stage of the cycle) it is important that the introduction of the changes is carefully planned. Pamela for instance will need to check handouts and worksheets to ensure that the language used is appropriate for the level of learner and that any technical terms are clearly explained. Syed will need to plan the timings of the learning activities closely if he is to spend longer with the lower level learners in the group. Julie has a considerable amount of detailed planning to do. She needs to look at the course programme to see how the project work might be restructured. For the individual sessions she needs to ensure that she has the roles ready for each individual trainee. If he is to tackle health and safety issues in every workshop session,

Alan will have to concentrate on individual session plans to ensure that the appropriate learning activity and associated learning materials have been included.

Reflection 2 – evaluation

It is best to undertake this reflection as soon as possible after the implementation of the changes so that the experience is fresh in the mind. Writing down reflections is helpful as it is a record that can be referred back to, useful if the teacher is dealing with a number of issues, which is usually the case!

There are several questions our teachers will ask themselves at this stage. The first will be: 'did the changes I implemented work?' A second question might be: 'if the changes did not work, why not?' The third is likely to be: 'what further changes do I need to make?' The asking of this question is an acknowledgement that the reflective cycle is not a closed one, and that reflecting on practice is an ongoing process.

In reflecting upon the changes she made Pamela considers that they have on the whole worked. The revisions she has made to teaching and learning materials have meant that the students can more readily make the links between psychological theory and their own practice in the workplace. Pamela has found however that there are still at least two students who are struggling with psychological concepts, and she is now planning how best she might offer them support.

Syed had mixed fortunes with the changes he implemented. He found that the group responded well to the revisiting of ground rules, and individual learners are now more likely to 'wait their turn'. He has however found that giving the lower level learners an extra ten minutes is not enough to give them the support they need, and he now looking at the learning materials he uses with these learners to see if changes there offer a solution.

Julie made the changes to the programme structure to concentrate the project into one week. This she has found has reduced the problems associated with trainee absences. She felt that she was less successful with the management of the group work. She has concluded that the problem might not be the roles *per se* but that the trainees need to develop team work skills. She is now working on activities to develop these skills before the trainees start the project work.

Alan has included an activity on health and safety in each of the motor vehicle workshop sessions, and in reflecting on several weeks of classes feels that there is an overall improvement in safe working practices, and therefore less chance of an accident. He does however have two concerns: first that the learners may become used to having an activity on health and safety at the start of each session and 'switch off', and second that there tends to be a rush to put tools away at the end of a session, increasing the risk of an accident. Alan is giving some thought to more activities that he can include at different times in a workshop session, and he is looking at the timings in his session and considering allowing more time to put tools away and tidy up.

It is at this point it becomes clear why there is an arrow at the top of Figure 2.1 above. It is rare in the practice of teaching that an issue is resolved all at once. The examples given of our four teachers illustrate that there will have to be at least some 'fine tuning', and in many cases a re-think on how an issue is to be tackled. There is however a more fundamental reason why the cycle is not closed. As stated in the introduction to this book, reflecting on practice is an ongoing process – there will always be other issues to be resolved! You will be introduced to several models of reflection later in this book, but you already have here a reflective tool that you can use on a daily basis in your professional practice.

Getting started with reflective writing

Reflective writing is a subject in itself and indeed has its own literature: see for instance the useful guide written by Moon (2006). A consideration of reflective writing is included here because it is an integral part of the reflective process, and it is more often than not a requirement on an initial teacher training course to keep a reflective journal on one's professional practice. Many student teachers find it difficult to get started writing reflectively, but it is our experience that it is an ability that develops over time. We have found that adopting a 'structured' approach to reflective writing in the early stages helps to develop confidence and fluency. Perhaps the easiest way to get begin is to start with the practice of teaching and enabling learning and then to divide it into its various aspects thus:

- planning for teaching and learning;
- teaching and learning strategies;
- teaching and learning resources and materials;
- classroom/workshop management issues;
- assessment of learning.

The process of reflective writing then starts with the teacher asking themselves a series of questions under the above headings and writing down the answers to the questions they have posed themselves:

Planning for teaching and learning

- Did I clearly identify the learning outcomes for the session?
- Did I plan for the differentiation of learning to meet individual learning needs?
- Did I get the timings of the various learning activities right?
- Did I have the right teaching and learning resources to hand and in sufficient quantity?
- Were the learning outcomes identified for the session achieved?

Teaching and learning strategies

- Were the teaching and learning methods used appropriate for the topic(s)?
- How effective were the methods in helping to achieve the stated learning outcomes for the session?
- What other teaching and learning methods might I have used in this session?

Teaching and learning resources and materials

- Did all the resources work properly?
- Did I select the right resources and materials to help achieve the outcomes for the session?
- Was the language used on PowerPoint presentations, handouts and worksheets appropriate for the level of the group?
- Did I make the necessary adjustments to materials and resources to take account of individual learning needs and/or disabilities?

Classroom/workshop management

- Did I start the session promptly?
- Were latecomers dealt with in an appropriate manner?
- Were the learners actively involved throughout the session?
- Was inappropriate learner behaviour satisfactorily dealt with?

Assessment of learning

- Did I take the opportunity to assess prior learning?
- Did I use appropriate methods to assess learner knowledge, skill and understanding?

Reflective writing is a topic we will return to later in the book when we consider critical incident analysis and how writing reflectively might help us understand the wider influences at work on professional practice and how we might respond to them.

3

Levels and models of reflective practice

Now that you have some knowledge of what a reflective cycle is we want to build on that knowledge and introduce *levels* of reflection and some *models* of reflection.

Levels of reflection

We suggest that there are three distinct but not mutually exclusive levels of reflection. They are:

1   *technical*: the reflection undertaken on a day to day basis by the teacher on their own practice in the classroom, workshop, salon, etc;
2   *organizational*: the reflection on the management and deployment of learning resources, activities and learner support;
3   *critical*: the reflection on the wider social, political and economic contexts within which the teacher work.

Technical reflection

This is the reflection that the teacher undertakes on their own teaching. It is concerned with the 'techniques' of planning teaching and learning, teaching and learning strategies, the use of teaching and learning resources, assessing learning and supporting individual learners. It is likely that the teacher will reflect on the following aspects of their own practice:

- *The planning and preparation of learning*   Here the teacher may consider the statement of the aims and objectives on the session plan: were they clear and specific enough? Were the individual and group learning needs identified? Then there is the consideration of the sequencing of topics and learning activities: was the ordering logical, would the teacher change it next time? Where the teaching and learning resources and materials are concerned the teacher will reflect on whether they were the right ones and whether they were available in sufficient quantities. Health and safety issues are also likely to be reflected on, for instance had the appropriate risk assessments been undertaken?

- *The introduction of the learning session* The teacher is likely to reflect on whether the aims and objectives for the session had been communicated to the learners, and whether as a result they understood what was expected of them. For many teachers there will also be the consideration of whether strong enough links have been made between prior learning and that in the session, for instance how effective the recap of learning was.

- *Communication* This concerns communication between the teacher and the learner and between the learners. The teacher will consider whether the volume and tone was appropriate for the learning environment – for instance could they be heard by all the learners? There is likely to be reflection on the quality of written communication, for instance on the whiteboard or flipchart. Where inter-learner communication is concerned, the teacher may consider the interaction during small group work and during learner presentations of their work.

- *Group management* There is likely to be reflection on how confidently and fairly behavioural issues were dealt with. There is likely to be a consideration of why such issues arise: is the learning engaging all individuals in the group? Are there issues of relevance of learning? Is the learning too difficult for an individual learner, or not challenging enough?

- *Teaching and learning methods* The teacher will reflect on the appropriateness of the methods in helping achieve the objectives set for the session and meeting the learning needs of both the group and individual learners within it. There is also likely to be a consideration of how far the selection and the use of the methods promoted active learning.

- *Teaching and learning resources* As with methods, the teacher is likely to reflect on the extent to which the resources used in the session aided the achievement of the stated objectives. The teacher may also reflect on whether certain resources functioned correctly, e.g personal computers or indeed whether the teacher had the necessary skills to use resources! (e.g. the electronic board).

- *Assessment and feedback* The teacher may reflect upon the use of assessment methods used in the session, for instance the use of question and answer technique and how effective the methods used in the assessment of learner knowledge and understanding were. Did the feedback given to learners on their performance and/or progress help improve knowledge and skills?

- *Differentiation of learning* How effective was any differentiation on the basis of ability of learner or content of the learning in meeting individual learning needs?

Organizational

At this level the teacher will reflect upon how teaching and learning is *organized* in the institution where they work. This is different from the reflection undertaken at the 'technical' level, because it involves considering the decisions taken by others as well as oneself on a range of issues that have an influence on the quality of teaching and learning.

- *Course organization*   It would be fair to say that most teachers teach their subject as part of a course rather than a series of 'one-offs'. They are likely to teach a series of sessions on a discrete course, for example 'Introduction to Spanish' or as part of a larger course, for example 'Costing and budgeting' on a business studies course. How the course is organized will have an impact on the professional practice of the individual teacher. Issues here might include a consideration of the timetabling of the course, the arrangement of the teaching and learning activities or the length of time given to the various activities. An example might be the reflection of a teacher on the balance of classroom and workshop activities on an engineering course.

- *Teaching and learning activities*   This is a wider consideration of teaching and learning than that which the individual teacher engages in. The nature of the activities in other course team members' sessions will of course have an influence. For example the teacher might reflect on a colleague's, teaching which is engaging and motivating the learners, to seek to incorporate some of that good practice in their own teaching. Conversely the teacher may reflect on the teaching and learning activities on the course and consider that there may be room for improvement, for instance making the learners more active than passive in the learning activities. As a result of this reflection the teacher may have suggestions that can be put to colleagues on the planning and conduct of learning activities.

- *Teaching and learning resources*   Here the teacher might reflect upon the quality, quantity and access to teaching and learning resources. There may be reflection on the quality of the learning environment: is the room 'fit for purpose'? For instance it is difficult to have small group activities in a lecture theatre. Another quality issue might be a resource commonly found in the learning environment, personal computers. Are they all working? Do they have the appropriate software loaded? The teacher may consider the number and amount of resources made available. Are there enough personal computers for the number in the group for instance? Finally the teacher will reflect on access to resources – are they readily to hand, or does the storage of them cause problems of access?

- *Learner support*   Are individual learners receiving the appropriate help with their learning needs and disabilities? There may be a consideration here of how learner support, for instance for literacy and numeracy, is provided and how it integrates with the course of study the learning is embarked upon. Could the teacher work more closely with those providing the support to make it more effective and relevant for the learner?

Critical

Beyond the organizational factors which impinge upon the professional practice of the teacher in the wider FE sector, there is the influence of the social, political and economic contexts on teaching and learning. Several writers on the wider FE sector, for instance Avis (1999) Hodkinson (1998) and Suter (2007) argue that government policy decisions on the organization and funding of the sector have had a major impact on the teacher's role, often increasing the workload and increasing levels of managerial supervision. Even so, research undertaken on learning cultures in further education colleges (James and Biesta 2007) found that the professionalism and creativity of teachers was central to the success of learners in all the colleges and all the courses researched. It could be argued then that teachers are still a major stakeholder in education and training and that it is reasonable that they should seek to understand the wider influences on their professional practice and to form a view on how those influences impact upon their work.

At this level the teacher is likely to reflect upon the policy decisions which affect the group of learners with whom they work. Thus for instance the teacher who works with young people will reflect upon the education and training policies for 14- to 19-year-olds and the provision, funding and qualification framework for this age group. The teacher who works with adult learners will reflect on the policy context as it affects those learners. Through this reflection the teacher will form a *critical* view of the wider influences on professional practice.

Models of reflective practice

Five models have been chosen to explore how various writers on reflection have understood the process and its applications, and how those models might be used to reflect on the professional practices in teaching. We start with Dewey, who might be considered one of the first in modern times to argue for the centrality of reflection in teaching and learning, and his 'stages of reflection'. Then there is a consideration of a writer working in the tradition of Dewey – Boud, and his model of reflective learning. The third is the work of another writer influenced by Dewey, Schön's 'reflection in action – reflection on action' model. The last two models relate directly to the practice of teaching, the 'critical incidents' model of Tripp and that of the 'critical lenses' model of Brookfield. These models have been included in the discussion because as their names suggest, they introduce the element of 'criticality' into reflective practice.

Dewey

There will be a consideration of Dewey's theories on education and training in Chapter 9, so here we will confine ourselves to his stages of reflection, as set out in his book *How We Think* (1933). He states that there are five 'distinct steps' in reflection:

1   a felt difficulty;
2   its location and definition;
3   suggestion of possible solution;
4   'development by reasoning of the suggestion;
5   further experiment leading to its acceptance or rejection.

Step one Dewey notes that a 'difficulty' arises when there is a 'Conflict between conditions at hand and a desired and intended result, between an end and the means for reaching it' (p. 72). This 'felt difficulty' can be readily contextualized in a teaching and learning situation. 'A desired and intended result' could be for instance the achievement of the stated learning outcomes for a learning session, or on an organizational level the setting up of a new course. 'Conditions at hand' might include the levels of motivation (or lack of it) of the learners, ability and attainment and the amount of time available for the learning. Organizational issues will include the resources available to run the course, funding, classrooms, workshops and staffing, as well as the interest of colleagues and management. The problem to be solved as Dewey saw it was: 'The discovery of intervening terms which when inserted between the remote end and the given means will harmonise them with each other' (p. 72).

To do this, we must first ascertain the nature of the 'felt difficulty':

Step two 'definition of the difficulty' This is a crucial step according to Dewey; it makes the difference between 'reflection proper' and 'uncontrolled thinking'. Dewey warns that at this stage it is important to suspend judgement and not reach any hasty conclusions as to what is the cause of the difficulty. Any rushing to a conclusion will result in any suggestions for a resolution of the problem being merely 'random'. An example in a teaching and learning context might be where a teacher is experiencing difficulties with learners' behaviour and concluding that it is because they lack motivation. To reach that conclusion at once, without considering other issues in the learning environment may result in the actual reason and therefore the possible solution to the difficulty being missed.

Step three 'suggestion' Dewey stated that synonyms for this word were 'conjecture' and 'hypothesis'. This is the stage where the various 'definitions' of the problem arrived at in step two are subject to more rigorous thought. Here the teacher gives consideration to a number of reasons for the problems with learner behaviour – are they involved enough in the learning? Are there problems with learners understanding the content?

Step four 'Development by reasoning' Through a process of careful thought some of the suggestions made at step three are dismissed. What is left is an idea or 'conjecture' which can be subject to what Dewey termed 'verification'.

Step five 'observation and experiment' This is where the idea or conjecture arrived at the end of step four is subject to 'direct observation' or 'experiment'. A teacher who has given careful thought to problems of a lack of learner engagement might consider that the problem is learner passivity in her classes. This conjecture can be tested by introducing more active learning into her sessions to see if that provides a solution.

Dewey offers us a systematic approach to reflection, one which addresses the uncertainties and complexities of human action, and one which has an application for the professional practice of teaching.

Schön

Schön (1983; 1987) avowedly worked in the tradition of Dewey in emphasizing the uncertainties inherent in human decision making. He described the complexities of professional practices including teaching and how professionals deal with them. Schön was critical of what is termed 'technical-rationalism', the idea that the 'one best way' is found to undertake a task, and then this prescription is followed at all times and in all circumstances. He argued that professional practices are complex, contingent and even 'messy', and so do not lend themselves to that 'technical' approach much influenced by 'systems' and 'behaviourists' theories. This is a particularly important point where teaching is concerned because of the great influence behaviourism continues to have on professional practice (Armitage et al. 2007).

If we accept that professional practices including that of teaching are complex, where there a lot of uncertainties and there is no 'off the peg' guide to tell us the right thing to do in every circumstance, how do we proceed? For Schön, the professional is knowledgeable in a unique way and demonstrates through 'reflection in action', practical or personal knowledge, what he called 'knowing in action'. The practical knowledge, reflecting in action, can been described as the teacher 'thinking on her or his feet', being spontaneous, creative and unique. According to Schön (1983), the professional exhibits a kind of artistry, building up a repertoire of knowledge and skills through reflection in action. Thus for instance a repertoire is built up by the teacher gaining understandings of situations in the learning environment to inform her or his actions. What then is the process of reflecting in action? Following Dewey, Schön sees the practitioner experiencing 'puzzlement 'or 'confusion' in a situation and an 'experiment' is carried out generate a new understanding of the situation. Thus a teacher will learn a range of classroom management skills, or an understanding when learners are finding a topic difficult, by 'experimenting' with different ways of dealing with these situations. If these prove to be successful, they will be added to the repertoire.

For Schön, the 'knowing in action' which results from building up a repertoire of skills is only the first part of reflective practice. 'Thinking on our feet' can be built upon through 'reflection on action'. This is done later, after the professional encounter, in the case of teachers the encounter with their learners. Reflection on action may involve writing up reflections, or discussing our professional practice with a mentor or colleagues. It enables a teacher to 'slow things down' (Schön 1987) to explore what happened and why it happened. This allows the teacher to develop sets of questions about their practice and develop further ideas for future practice.

It is easy to see why Schön's model of reflective practice has been so influential in teacher education. First, there is an acknowledgement of the complexities of teaching, and the need to build a repertoire of knowledge and skills over a period of time to deal with the many varied situations in which a teacher will find themselves. It is the 'reflection on action' which means it is not merely learning 'the tricks of the trade'; it is subjecting one's practice to systematic, sustained thought.

Boud, Keogh and Walker's experiential model of reflection

Boud et al.'s model (1985) is, like Schön's, constructed in the tradition of Dewey. They state that the impetus to reflect may come about because of a 'loss of confidence' or 'disillusionment' in one's situation (p. 19), though reflection might also be 'prompted' by more positive experiences, like successfully completing a difficult task. For Boud et al. reflection is a response to experience. There are therefore two parts to the model: first the experience itself and second the reflection which is based on that experience (p. 18) This experience may be 'formal learning', for example on a course of study, or it could be as Boud et al. put it 'a totally unplanned occurrence in daily life'. There is an acknowledgement that learning can take place in a less formal way, in the workplace for example.

There are three stages in Boud et al.'s model, 'returning to experience', 'attending to feelings' and 'returning to experience'. In stage one there is a recollection of what took place, either that which has caused a 'loss of confidence' or more positively a recent success. Boud et al. note that as one begins to 'replay the experience' details start to emerge which were ignored at the time of the experience. It is only when we deliberately seek to reflect on our experiences that these details come to light. This deliberation also ensures that the reflection is based on 'real events' rather than 'what we wished had happened' (p. 28). An example might be the teacher who has had a fraught experience introducing a new topic to her learners. During the session several learners complain that it is 'boring' and not relevant. In reflecting on the experience our teacher considers that this was the first time that she had introduced a topic with an element of numeracy, in this case working out averages, and that a significant number of learners had struggled with the calculations. Boud et al. write of a 'stepping back' from experience; because one does not have to act or react to experience in 'real time', there is the opportunity to view the experience from a variety of perspectives, including that of others who were involved in the experience. At this stage the reflection should be 'clear of any judgements' as this may cause one to miss some features of the experience that were important.

Boud et al. named stage two 'attending to feelings'. Though they acknowledge that there are working in the tradition of Dewey, they state that they give much greater emphasis to the 'affective aspects of learning' (p. 21). They place this emphasis on emotional feelings for two reasons. First they can become 'barriers to learning' – they can 'override our rationality' (p. 28). The second reason is that 'positive feelings' can be used to provide us with the 'impetus to persist' in challenging situations. Reflecting upon positive experiences of success at a task can lead to the feelings of self- worth and confidence necessary to continue with a difficult task. Returning to feelings as 'barriers' Boud et al. argue that they need to be 'discharged' or 'transformed' to enable one to respond effectively to a situation (p. 29) They suggest that this process may involve discussing the situation in a 'supportive environment' or through reflective writing. The teacher in our example had been greatly upset by the reaction of some of the learners in that session and made her doubt her ability to introduce any element of numeracy into her teaching. She was able to discuss her feelings with colleagues and thus voice her anxieties.

The third and final stage is that of 're-evaluating the experience'. This in turn is split into four elements: 'association', 'integration', 'validation' and 'appropriation'. For Boud et al. 'association' is the linking of the ideas and feelings of both the original experience and reflection with existing knowledge and attitudes, the start of a learning process. This they say can challenge one 'intellectually and affectively' (p. 31). It may lead to a reassessment of old attitudes, and that one's earlier knowledge needs to be modified in the light of the new. Boud et al. note that these associations can be 'indiscriminate'; that there needs to be a further examination to see whether they are likely to be useful. They call this stage 'integration' because it is where new knowledge and feelings can be integrated into a 'new whole'. They suggest that this process can be aided by writing thoughts down and making connections between the new and existing knowledge and feelings. The next element is 'validation', where the knowledge and feelings we have started to integrate is subject to a 'reality test'. Here one is testing for consistency between the new and the old knowledge, and trying out the new knowledge in new situations. 'Appropriation' is the last element at this stage. This is where the new knowledge becomes so important to someone that it becomes part of their 'value system' (p. 34). Boud et al. state that not all new knowledge is appropriated, but that when it is it can be difficult to change, and it is for that reason care should be taken to process and integrate new knowledge. In our example the teacher realizes that she needs to change the way she introduces any element of numeracy to the group as there are obviously issues of ability and confidence. She knows she will have to adopt a differentiated approach, offering challenge to those most able in numeracy, and more support to the less able and confident. She introduces the topic again, taking care to establish the relevance of the topic and adopting teaching and learning strategies that will offer both challenge to the more able and support to the less able. Over time these differentiated approaches become an established part of her repertoire of teaching and learning strategies.

Boud et al. are careful to point out that reflection in itself is not enough. The new learning must be put into action (p. 35). It could be argued that engaging in activity based upon the new knowledge learned through reflection is a continuing 'testing of reality' on which in turn one might reflect. Boud et al. state that there is a 'continuing cycling back and forth between elements'. Reflective learning is an ongoing process.

Tripp's critical incidents theory

This is the first of two theories of reflective practice notable for being concerned with the professional practice of teaching. Tripp (1993) argues that teachers need to explore the incidents that occur in the everyday work of the professional practice of teaching. A questioning of their own practice enables teachers to develop an understanding of the processes of teaching, and crucially to develop professional judgement.

A critical incident in teaching is that which the teacher interprets as a challenge in their professional situation. Tripp states that when an incident occurs, the teacher needs to ask what happened and what caused it to happen. This is a crucial aspect of critical incident analysis; the framing of the questions that the teacher asks her or himself.

The first step is choosing the critical incident. The critical incident does not have to be dramatic; it might be an everyday event that occurs in the classroom and workshop, but is significant in that it might be indicative of underlying motives, structures and processes. What is crucial however is that the issue is important to the individual teacher concerned. For one teacher it might be an incident of learners arriving particularly late for a class which starts the process of reflection, or a set of poor grades for a learner assessment. It might be more dramatic like an incident of unruly behaviour in the classroom or workshop. The teachers in all these cases start the process of reflection on the critical incident to discover reasons for the incident and hopefully to improve the situation.

Having chosen a critical incident, the teacher gives a careful description of it:

- Who was involved?
- Where did it happen?
- What actually happened?
- What the teacher's reaction to the incident?

When the description is made, the next stage is the analysis of the incident. The first question to ask is 'why' the incident happened. Is it the learning environment itself, the classroom or workshop? It might be related to the learners, something to do with the nature of the group, the ability and attainment levels or their motivation to learn. It might not be the group *per se* but individuals within it. The incident may be related to the subject or topic.

Let us take as an example a teacher who has chosen as her critical incident the absence of learners from a course assessment. She sets out by describing the incident – six of the 20 learners absented themselves without notice from a two hour 'open book' examination which forms part of a course assessment. The teacher might start by asking herself questions about the nature of the assessment: did the fact that it was an 'examination' cause anxiety among those learners? Considering her own role in the incident, had she prepared the learners adequately for the assessment? She may consider the background of the learners: could it be that relatively low levels of educational attainment in the past have resulted in a lack of confidence? Here the teacher begins to ask herself questions relating to what Tripp described as 'social' or 'structural' issues, an attempt reach an understanding of how the wider societal context of education and training impacts upon professional practice. If they are learners who had poor attainment at school it might have resulted in lower expectations of success and lower self-esteem. The teacher might even ask herself whether the issue might be with the assessment instrument itself. Do the students *have* to be assessed that way?

When the teacher in our example has considered the questions s/he has framed for herself on the critical incident, the analysis continues with the question of what can be learned from the incident and ends with what can be done to find a resolution.

As with Boud et al. Tripp is careful to point out that reflection is a cyclical process (p. 32). Tripp's reflective cycle starts with the observation of a situation out of which the teacher 'creates' the critical incident. The teacher then plans a response before implementing that response. This is followed by an observation of the effects of the response before going on to create another critical incident.

Brookfield's 'critical reflection'

Brookfield begins mounting his case for critical reflection in teachers with the statement that 'teaching can never be 'innocent' (1995: 1). Innocence according to Brookfield is the thinking that teachers always understand what they are doing and what effect our teaching is having. Further, it is an assumption that the meanings and significance that teachers put on their actions are the ones the learners put on them. Brookfield argues that this innocence is at best naïve, and at worst it is damaging. He argues that we can never have full awareness of our motives and intentions, and we can misinterpret the way others perceive our actions. This Brookfield states 'sets us up for a 'lifetime of frustration'.

Brookfield (1995) argues the problems caused by innocence in teaching can be avoided if teachers are prepared to question their assumptions through a process of critical reflection He states that teachers' reflection on practice should be a process of 'hunting assumptions', where assumptions are the 'taken for granted' beliefs about the world (1995: 2). Brookfield identifies three sets of assumptions:

- *Paradigmatic assumptions*   According to Brookfield these are the most difficult assumptions to uncover. They are the structuring assumptions we use to order the world into different categories, and crucially we can think that they are an objective view of reality, and so are difficult to question and change. Brookfield gives the example of the assumption that adults are self-directed learners, something he came to question through reflection on practice.
- *Prescriptive assumptions*   These are what we think *ought* to happen in a given situation. This set of assumptions, Brookfield notes, is grounded in the paradigmatic assumptions; thus if we believe that adults are self-directed learners we will have assumptions about how adults ought to approach their learning.
- *Causal assumptions*   This is the relationship between a cause and effect: if x does something, y will happen. Brookfield uses the example of learning contracts, for example, that if a teacher uses these with learners, they will become more independent in their learning.

The above sets of assumptions can be 'hunted' by teachers if they are prepared to view their practice through four 'critical lenses':

- The first is our autobiographies as learners and teachers. Through a process of reflection on their own learning and professional practice a teacher becomes aware of the paradigmatic assumptions that influence the way they teach.
- The second is teachers looking at their practice through their learners' eyes. According to Brookfield, this allows a teacher to check whether the learners are taking from the teaching that they intend.
- The third is colleagues' experiences. Brookfield argues that a teacher inviting colleagues to observe their practice, and engaging in 'critical conversations' with them, notices aspects of professional practice normally hidden to them.
- The fourth is theoretical literature. This helps to 'inform' a teacher's practice. Brookfield argues that it provides the teacher with 'multiple perspectives' on familiar situations. There are now a considerable number of journals specializing in the LLS or aspects of teaching and learning, for instance information and computer technology in education and training.

Brookfield not only offers a model of reflective practice in teaching, but also a clear rationale for engaging in critical reflection (pp. 24–6):

- It helps us take informed actions. Brookfield argues that an informed action has a better chance of achieving the consequence intended.

- It helps us develop a rationale for practice. The teacher is able to justify to others, particularly learners and colleagues, the reasons for our actions in our professional practice.

- It helps us avoid self-laceration, and to acknowledge that as teachers we are not responsible for everything that goes wrong. Brookfield notes a tendency in teachers to take responsibility for everything!

- It grounds us emotionally. It helps the teacher achieve an emotional balance in their professional practice.

- It enlivens our classrooms. Brookfield states that seeing a teacher model critical enquiry is helpful to the learner to think critically.

- It increases democratic trust. According to Brookfield the critically reflective teacher gives careful consideration to the learner's 'voice' in the learning environment, showing that the relationship with the learners is important to them, thus increasing their trust in the teacher.

What do these five models have in common? In all of them there is an acknowledgement that the world is a fast-changing, complicated place, and what we learn of it is necessarily contingent and has to be subject to continual review. The professional practice of teaching is not an exception. Each of the models has something to offer the teacher reflecting on their practice. Dewey was the first to emphasize reflection as being a systematic process. Schön developed this by stating that experience needed to be 'slowed down' in a process of reflection on action. Boud et al. acknowledged their debt to Dewey but also emphasized the need to take the 'emotional' element of learning into account. Tripp provides a *focus* for reflecting on practice by his emphasis on the teacher identifying 'critical incidents' and reflecting on them. Brookfield provides us with the *perspectives* from which to reflect on practice, not only the teacher's own, but also that of the learners and colleagues. Further, he argues that our practice should be informed by the relevant literature on teaching and learning. Finally, Brookfield is valuable in that he provides us with a clear rationale for *why* teachers should engage in professional practice.

4
Collaborative reflective practice

The benefits of collaborative reflective practice (observing and being observed by, and working and discussing with, like-minded peers) can be expansive and highly developmental. Here we get to see and hear what others are using, the subtle ways they negotiate the chemistry of a session and the strategies that they employ to sort out the particular challenges and nuances of their context at a critical level. While these insights help us to make informed judgements about what might work, or prohibit learning, in our sessions they can also reinforce and fortify our uncertainties about what we have tried in the past, give us a voice and promote the building of strong personal and professional relationships among peers. Thus, we suggest that the social learning theories of Vygotsky et al. (1978) are as valuable for teachers as they are for learners.

The fragmented nature of a teacher's life in the LLS means that we often work on our own yet surrounded by those in our 'community of practice' which Lave and Wenger seminally describe as follows:

> In using the term community, we do not imply some primordial culture-sharing entity. We assume that members have different interests, make diverse contributions to activity, and hold varied viewpoints. In our view, participation at multiple levels is entailed in membership in a community of practice. Nor does the term community imply necessarily co-presence, a well defined identifiable group, or socially visible boundaries. It does imply participation in an activity system about which participants share understandings concerning what they are doing and what this means in their lives and for their communities.
>
> (Lave and Wenger 1991: 97–8)

Such a definition offers the notion that those in our communities of practice may include teaching colleagues with the same or similar subject specialism, those in other teams who teach on similar programmes or work with similar levels of learners, those in other organizations who we network with, other trainee teachers (the benefits to trainees of team teaching or observing other contexts are enormous), our stakeholders (those who have a vested interest in what we do, for example employers), and those we engage with at a distance through professional or social networks. Trainee teachers should also have at least one subject specialist mentor 'nearby' and it is often particularly beneficial to have a mentor who is remote from the team or organization (see Chapter 5). Petty (1993: p 361) reminds us of the value of a mentor or other subject specialist where, 'Asking for advice is not an admission of failure, but evidence of your desire to succeed.'

Sadly, some colleagues prefer to work in isolation either because they have uncertainties about showing too much of themselves or because organizational and cultural structures have not enabled collaboration in the past. We suggest that such hitherto untapped colleagues can be a fruitful harvest ground since our peers feel valued when asked, when unexpectedly given a voice and when suddenly invigorated to understand themselves and their practice better. Likewise, our institutions are often unclear about how to develop our 'dual professional' (Orr and Simmons 2009) skill sets as they work on changing each of us from a trained and experienced vocational or subject specialist into a teacher.

Yet we also caution the belief that collaboration for its own sake can be an inefficient use of time and effort. For example, externally held CPD events often fail to scratch all teachers where they itch and internally held compulsory collaborative events (mandatory institution-wide CPD events) are sometimes used to implement organizational change that is either limiting or has a micro-political agenda. While these tend to be unavoidable, there is nothing wrong in you being selective about what you wish to get out of collaboration nor is it improper or unwelcome to grasp the opportunity and try to invigorate a deeper awareness or appreciation of teaching and learning throughout your community of practice and organization.

In this chapter we seek to illustrate a collaborative approach to reflective practice which dissolves structural barriers and hierarchies through three case studies.

Case study 1: curriculum evaluation and the self assessment report (SAR)

Paul is the team leader for the trowel trades (brickwork) section of a private training provider organization that specializes in construction trades. The organization is in competition with the local FE college in offering NVQ level 1 courses to school link groups and NVQ levels 2 and 3 to apprentices in the local area. The organization is Skills Funding Agency (SFA) and (Young People's Learning Agency YPLA) funded (and therefore the annual SAR is a mandatory document to be produced for such organizations), subject to Ofsted inspection, has an effective self-assessment regime for its provision and maintains links with the local construction industry through a cross-disciplinary team of workplace OSAT (On-Site Assessment and Training) assessors. The provision had grown dramatically over the previous five years resulting in two new tutors being recruited from industry in the previous two years bringing the team to five, including Paul, and using the whole of one building on the site. All five teach both theory and workshop practical sessions and are observed twice each academic year by the organization's quality assurance manager. Paul encourages informal mentoring within the team although they tend not to mix on a daily basis with teams based in other buildings since there tends to be a competitive, occasionally hostile, ethos between disciplines.

As team leader Paul had, throughout the year, maintained a keen overview of programme files and the relevant documentation required for the SAR at the end of the year although he felt that his team should take more ownership of the SAR, both the writing of it and the areas for improvement. Taken as a whole, the SAR is an evaluative and analytical review of a programme based on five key questions (KQs):

- KQ1 How well do learners achieve?
- KQ2 How effective are teaching, training and learning?
- KQ3 How well do programmes and activities meet the needs and interest of learners?
- KQ4 How well are learners guided and supported?
- KQ5 How effective are leadership and management in raising achievement and supporting all learners?

Upon completion of KQ1 (statistical data regarding how well learners achieve), which Paul did on his own, he had to acknowledge that while the data was at or above national benchmarks for the last five years with an upward trend for the first four years, the data for level 2 and 3 learners had hit a plateau in the current year. Given the organization's preference for Paul's curriculum manager to lead the writing for KQ5 (how effective are leadership and management in raising achievement and supporting learners?) in collaboration with individual team leaders, Paul wanted his team to collaborate in answering the three remaining KQs.

Paul arranged a half day team review in one of the classrooms, with the promise of culminating in a pub lunch, at which he gave the findings of his work on KQ1, the gist of which was that they continued to do well but that the growth trend had levelled off. He explained that he wanted to protect the five jobs and stay ahead of the neighbouring college but, despite local expansion in the construction industry, he also wanted to know his team's thoughts on why, according to the data, they appeared to have peaked. To help them he had also invited an experienced member of the OSAT team, the brickwork technician, a learning support worker (LSW) seconded to construction and his ex-tutor from the teacher education department. Three tables were set apart, one for each KQ, and included the following paper-based data:

KQ2 table: How effective are teaching, training and learning?

- 10 internal QA session observation forms (with permission of the five teachers):
  - three grade 1
  - five grade 2
  - two grade 3

KQ3 table: How well do programmes and activities meet the needs and interests of learners?

- a range of OSAT evidence including employer feedback and evaluations;
- candidate monitoring reports and Individual Learning Plans (ILPs) (all level 2 and 3 groups);

- group tracking sheets (all groups);
- SPOC (student perception of college) analysis (one for each term);
- end of course evaluations (all groups);
- NVQ External Verifier report;

KQ4 table: How well are learners guided and supported?

- tutorial files (all groups);
- two focus group reports carried out by a member of the senior management team (level 2 and 3 groups);
- tutorial and enrichment programmes.

Staff were distributed as follows. Each experienced tutor was paired with one of those recently recruited, Paul was paired with the technician, the teacher educator would remain at the KQ2 table, the OSAT assessor would remain at the KQ3 table and the LSW would remain at the KQ4 table.

Paul's brief to the teachers was to:

- appraise the available data;
- suggest any missing or additional data or evidence;
- think about what the data is not saying;
- think about what the data says regarding the learner experience;
- think about how learners' personal development can be better/more accurately measured;
- find out what we are doing well;
- find out what we can/should/could do better;
- be critical yet constructive.

As a prompt to invigorate reflective practice, the teacher educator was tasked with using Socratic questioning to elicit the staff's thoughts on what the KQ2 data amounted to when visiting that table; the OSAT assessor was to question each pair about the relationship, perceived or assumed, between the KQ3 data and their teaching roles; and the LSW was to question them about the extent and impact of the current support of learners. Each pair were to spend 30 minutes at each table, make their own notes and summarize the strengths, areas for development and any other key points on flip charts (three from each pair at each table) before moving to the next table. At the end of the activity Paul sent the four teachers and the technician to make coffee while he de-briefed the three table hosts; their initial comments were as follows:

KQ2: How effective are teaching, training and learning?

The teachers appreciated seeing each others' observation forms and were encouraged that their own areas for development were echoed in the others – they gave a flavour of 'no longer feeling isolated', an emotion that Paul had been unaware of in the team. They also identified emerging themes from the observations: both grade 3 sessions were with the same group and had suffered due to minor disruption and inattentiveness in the sessions; both grade 3s and most of the grade 2s did not have sufficient variety in assessment methods, differentiation in stretching the more able could be improved and there was little evidence of tutor comments on marked work. In contrast, they were interested in why the grade 1 sessions had those same points listed as strengths and were somewhat puzzled by the comment, 'effective use of independent research to locate the learning outcomes to current vocational practices' on a grade 1 session. The table host was of the opinion that all the teachers reflected quite naturally on the evidence and left the table, 'happy but thinking hard'.

KQ3: How well do programmes and activities meet the needs and interest of learners?

For the OSAT assessor the exercise had been 'a revelation' since he had not realized how far out of touch the teaching staff were, including the recent recruits, regarding employers and the work of the OSAT team, particularly the tensions between employers and the organization, and the difficulties in capturing sufficient workplace evidence of trainee competence. They had spotted a number of disturbing trends in the employers' feedback where a number of employers had accused 'the college' of teaching out of date techniques, spending too long on health and safety, wasting time on 'maths and English' and being inaccessible to employers. Only the technician had given any indication that he agreed with the criticisms.

KQ4: How well are learners guided and supported?

The LSW was more measured in her comments which amounted to the teachers suffering from the belief that support was the remit of LSWs, not them, and that the programmes of enrichment and tutorial activities were irrelevant to brickwork. However, all staff had shown interest in the focus group reports where students had given a flavour of not having been given much by way of induction, had no idea what to do to improve their performance in written exams and felt that the numeracy was too difficult for what they did on building sites.

While the teacher educator, OSAT assessor and LSW got into a discussion about how functional skills are embedded and supported in the workplace, the flip charts were stuck to the walls in KQ categories (three of strengths, three of weaknesses and three of other key points), making 27 sets of immediate thoughts, as coffee arrived. Individually, the five teachers considered what the data was or was not saying, how the SAR would look, whether it was a fair representation of what they had assumed the learner experience to be and what the key findings were. Paul gave each teacher a blank copy of Table 4.1 to complete as a summary of the findings which were then compared before the actions were agreed.

At this point, the team seemed to have moved closer together, not least in their confidence to be open with each other, and Paul wanted to utilize this strength in agreeing ways in which they could move things forward so he summarized the tables as follows:

KQ2: How effective are teaching, training and learning?

That which is a strength is also something we need to develop – but the skills to do so are in the team. We have some isolated learner misbehaviour that needs to be checked – but we know what, why and where it is.

KQ3: How well do programmes and activities meet the needs and interest of learners?

There is a mismatch between what learners do here and at work – but we know that this could be due to employers thinking differently to us. If there was better communication between the tutors and employers then, maybe, these concerns would go away or be minimized. Likewise, OSAT are stuck in the middle firefighting while trying to capture NVQ evidence.

Table 4.1 Summary of KQ data

Strengths	**KQ2** How effective are teaching, training and learning? Three outstanding: Assessment; stretch; feedback; research.	**KQ3** How well do programmes and activities meet the needs and interest of learners? One tutor locates the learning within industry.	**KQ4** How well are learners guided and supported?
Weaknesses	Seven to improve: Assessment; stretch; feedback. Need to manage behaviour (isolated cases?)	Four tutors appear distant from industry. Quality of NVQ workplace evidence (?) Tensions with employers (their views): Dated techniques; excessive health & safety; functional skills; lack of tutor–employer communication.	Tutors do not have ownership of support (left to LSW). Tensions with learners (their views): Poor induction; lack of guidance for exams; maths is irrelevant (?)
Source	Observation forms.	Employer evaluations. Candidate monitoring forms. SPOC and end evaluations.	SPOC and end evaluations. Focus group reports.
Key points	Now aware of each others' teaching. Identified the group with behavioural issues.	There must be more strengths (?) Employers uninformed. Training provider uninformed.	Not a strength in sight. Why do we have to do enrichment and tutorial?
Actions			

KQ4: How well are learners guided and supported?

How do we turn this into a strength? Does more tutor support necessarily mean more time or is there an alternative? Why do students think the way they do – is it lack of communication again? What do we do about enrichment and tutorial?

It was agreed that these were fair summaries so Paul organized three different pairs and allocated them to one of the hosts with the brief:

1 Being pragmatic and taking into account all the constraints on us, especially time and resources, what actions can we realistically aim for?
2 How can we improve the learner experience?
3 How can we improve our teaching practice?
4 How can we involve/communicate more with employers?
5 How can we support learners better?

After discussions, in groups and between groups, the team offered the following:

KQ2: How effective are teaching, training and learning?

The teacher who received two outstanding grades offered to have the other tutors observe his sessions on an informal ad-hoc basis and to explain how he used learners' workplace evidence and experiences as research-based material. The teacher educator offered to run a one-off session for the whole construction department on managing challenging behaviour.

KQ3: How well do programmes and activities meet the needs and interest of learners?

Paul offered to write a team newsletter which would go out by email each half term to employers. All tutors volunteered to accompany the OSAT assessor during non-teaching days to build relationships with employers and learners. They thought it might also be a source of up to date CPD and resources for the team.

KQ4: How well are learners guided and supported?

All tutors accepted the LSW's invitation to work-shadow, ostensibly as extra support, her and a colleague in some of the level 2 and 3 vocational classes they worked in where they supported numeracy needs. She knew of one tutor in particular who provided detailed, encouraging and developmental feedback to learners 'in class' with apparent ease and effectiveness.

Paul offered to evaluate and radically overhaul the induction programme. At the end of each year, all learners would be asked to write a 'letter to next year's apprentices' explaining to them how they could benefit most from the course.

While there was still much to think about, the team felt that they had achieved something significant as they headed for lunch and the teacher educator claimed three hours CPD for the event.

Case study 2: involvement with an on-line specialist community to inform and enhance pedagogic practice

Tom is a trainee Sports Science trainer and the following extract is from the reflective log that he needs to maintain as part of his ITE course.

At this early stage of my Cert. Ed. course I am required to begin a reflective log through which I illustrate my work with other professionals in my subject specialism and which is in addition to the mentoring record in my PDP (Personal Development Plan).

Whilst I have never been a diarist, I feel that this will be useful since it is both new to me, will encourage me to think in a specialist strand (I've always taken my specialism, Sports Science, as a given), might help me to 'think forward' as well as back and will allow me to gather together a whole range of odd things that I've been keeping in a box file because I didn't know what else to do with them.

As this is my first entry I should give some brief background. I left school with few qualifications, but with a good record at all sports, and started at an FE college because it had reciprocal links with the local football club where I had undergone schoolboy trials. I never made the first team but got my BTEC National and did paid coaching for the club while developing work as a self-employed personal trainer. I currently have a 0.5 post teaching Sports Science at an all-male Category B prison, continue the personal training two days per week and act as a second physiotherapist (the paid physiotherapist is my mentor) for the football club at weekends.

On the Cert. Ed. we have been introduced to something called OurSubject which is a VLE with free resources, chat room and a network of others with the same specialism. This has been really useful as I have been sharing ideas with other sports trainers (two of whom are physiotherapists) and a second year student who teaches in prisons. Like him, I'm not able to take any electronic resources into prison nor are there any web facilities so it has been really useful swapping ideas with him about how to deliver the theory side of the programme. Because he's in the second year, he also has access to the Specialist Subject conference website that I'll be doing next year and he's told me about the conference paper that he's writing and what the other sports trainers in his group are doing. Most of the resources in the free resource bank require ICT facilities and a couple of these, especially the 'drag-and-drop' anatomical package that someone shared, have saved me time in preparing theory slots to the footballers and have engaged them as learners better than PowerPoints do. I have also adapted some of the PowerPoints for the gym training which has improved the quality of my personal training business. A lot of the posts that people leave seem a bit cautious and introductory but there is a distinct feeling that there are others who share our specialism worrying over the same things and I'm encouraged that I'm not on my own. There is a chat room but I haven't offered anything to that yet since I suspect it might be too 'social'.

I also found a 'buddy' (someone whose personal profile is a 93% match for my own) who teaches art and design in a similar prison although she doesn't miss the electronic facilities as much. It was interesting to hear the way her job has been re-structured recently and I'm doing some CPD (level 2 maths) as a result to bolster my CV in case we're next. I shared this with my second year on-line friend and he has decided to do a BA in Education and Professional Development as soon as he completes the Cert. Ed. for the same reason. I mentioned to my mentor that we never seem to stop learning and he confided that he's doing enhanced mentor training at the moment with a view to taking his coaching qualifications next year – there's more of it about than I thought.

Since starting my teaching role I've been keen to see how the other coaching professionals and trainers deliver their teaching, especially theory, at the football club. They know all about motivation and one of them told me he uses NLP (neuro linguistic programming) to make the players think positively. For example, he talks about 'when' rather than 'if' and 'will' rather than 'can' – really subtle ways of using language that I've started using in the gym with my clients. I've had less success with it in the prison but the learners there don't feel that they have much to look forward to most of the time. Maybe I should look it up on the University VLE and see how else it is used. At the club, I've noticed they also make frequent changes in activities and the ways in which small groups are formed (like differentiation) and I've started to do more of that in the prison practical sessions which they seem to like because it makes several 'new starts' rather than just one start at the beginning.

Case study 3: reflection on engagement with cross-contextual peers as part of institution-wide CPD

This third case study is a spontaneous reflective account by an experienced painting and decorating tutor of an institution-wide CPD event, in the form of an internal memo, to the event organizer. Here, Joe clearly identifies the benefits and tutor development gleaned through collaborative work with colleagues outside his own specialism when staff CPD is approached in innovative ways.

Memo

To: Samia Turner
From: Joe Roller
Re: Staff Development day

Hi Samia,
I'm not in the habit of writing letters but thought I'd comment on yesterday's mandatory end of year 'we're going to pretend that we don't know you all hate these' staff development day.

First, I was surprised that you've read Coffield's (2008) *Just Suppose Teaching and Learning Became the First Priority*, and taken it as the theme for the day. Second, there was a distinct feeling that the leadership have moved from having us live a life of calculation (stats etc) to joining us in the trenches, particularly the Head Mistress's speech which was much less of the usual 'You've all done well but you need to pull your fingers out next year' to one which seemed to have more of a vision. It was also encouraging to learn that all the SMT, including the Principal, will have a nominal teaching load from next term.

Third, well done in providing workshops that broke the normal diet, the particular high points of those I attended being:

Embedding Functional Skills Without Tears

Brilliant – the FS (functional skills) team pulled off the whole theme really well – modelling best practice (I can't remember numeracy being fun); excellent resources to take away and adapt; hands-on learning for us; and taking away great ideas for fixing something that I thought had more or less broken in our team since we dropped Basic Skills.

Sleepless in Scunthorpe

The Workforce Development team's efforts at capturing NVQ evidence for cleaning staff on the night shift (always reassuring to know that there's someone worse off than yourself) – really funny but they got us thinking about how we could do it differently in Painting and Decorating. E.g. the electronic stuff they have (mini-scanners, a stick that turns a canteen wall into a whiteboard, flip video cameras and a data projector the size of a fag packet) gave me ideas for the next capital bid – we could really turn up the quality of the evidence if we weren't carting around old kit and it would make the EV happy (always asking for video evidence).

Pedagogy in the Trenches

I had no idea what to expect from this, especially as it was one of the HE guys doing it, but it was really interesting in how he supports mature learners doing a degree in college. I'd heard of Brookfield before but didn't know that he did all that critical stuff about being different and I'd never heard of Trifonas or Freire but it got me thinking about how we can make a difference, especially with the difficult students that come to P&D because they think it's going to be arty and easy. Some of them have real issues outside college but I now think we can help with that, e.g. being more understanding about lateness or not doing homework – I'm going to think around how we can nail the self study when they're here and how tutorial and enrichment can be a bit more meaningful.

Differentiation for Dummies

I've always worried about this differentiation thing – people talk about it as though we all know what it means but we don't. 'Quality' is the same. We always do the learning styles questionnaires and accommodate all three in all our sessions but that's as far as it goes. The idea that differentiation should also challenge the smart students was news to me but makes sense. The best part was when Diane had us defining common education terms with the match cards – I've never worked so hard but it's given me an idea for my level 3 group (similar sets of cards, laminated and in my bag in case the quick ones finish early).

Employer Engagement (Mandatory workshop)

I have a serious distrust of the mandatory workshops – always about the next new thing that the college needs to address, but is foisted onto teachers to sort out. Well done for breaking the mould and I know that those sat near me thought the same.

The idea of updating skills/industry knowledge etc. through better links with employers was interesting. I mean, we phone employers daily (students absent or not bringing safety boots etc.) but we never get into looking at things from their perspective and the idea that, in doing so, we update our knowledge at the same time is useful. Some of them send us their end-of-range paint and paper etc., but we only come across the latest stuff through the trade journals. I thought it might be useful to get one of the specialist employers to get involved with the level 3 students (guest sessions/ master class for marbling etc?) and build it from there, e.g. what employers want us to do that we aren't already doing; what they think we should stop doing; how they can help us and their apprentices more from their end; how we can improve the learner experience through innovative resources; or how we can improve motivation (I'm thinking of an employer sponsoring a prize for apprentice of the year) and things like that.

One of the notable things to come out of the day was that everyone was talking and seemed to enjoy what they'd been doing (even Hair and Beauty had their lunch with the Childcare lot).

My only regret was that I didn't go to the Interactive White Board training (I've already done it three times but forgotten it all because my room doesn't have an IWB). According to one of the guys in Public Services, there was no presenter – just a list of task instructions that they all had to discuss between themselves and then work through by trial and error while being recording by a video camera at the back of the room, the footage of which would be uploaded onto the VLE. Five minutes before the end an ICT Champion turned up and asked them what they'd learnt, suggested that 'since you haven't broken it, why don't you let your students use these things?', picked up the video camera and left. I'm really looking forward to watching that.

In summary, thanks for a great day.

Practical activities

The following practical activities develop two themes concerned with collaborative reflective practice: the development of teaching and learning and their impact on the learner experience through collaboration with learners; and the development of a particular teaching skill through peer and organizational collaboration. Both activities have been designed to help you develop both collaborative and individual reflective skills in subtle and non-threatening ways.

Activity 1: learner experience

Choose a course you run and ask:
Yourself:
Who works hardest in the sessions, me or the learners?
　　How can I get them to work harder than me (or even harder if they already do)?

When you have two or three answers to the second question, further ask:

- What would be the benefits for them?
- What could they learn from each other?
- Could they assess each other informally?
- How would motivation be affected?
- Would there be sufficient stretch and challenge of the more able?
- Would there be support of the less able?
- Two other questions of your own:
  a)
  b)

Your learners:

- How would you prefer to learn what you need to know?
- What do you want from me?
- What do you want me to do more of?
- What do you want me to do less of?
- Two other questions from the learners:
  a)
  b)

When you have reflected on these, share your thoughts with the best teacher you know and ask for their immediate comments.

Finally, ask yourself Feuerstein et al.'s (1994) two killer questions:

1   What is the process you have just gone through?
2   How could you apply that process elsewhere?

Activity 2: skill development

Identify one of the following teaching skills that you would like to develop:

- critical questioning: checking learners' understanding of a concept, having them relate it to their context and to other concepts, and extending their knowledge;
- exploiting learners as research: how to embed learners' personal and work experiences in taught sessions to promote whole group learning;
- developmental feedback: giving in-class verbal feedback which both recognizes achievement and makes clear how learners can develop further;
- peer learning: structured paired or small group work where learners learn from, and support, each other.

Contact the person in charge of Quality systems (who oversees internal graded observations of teaching and learning) in your organization and explain that you have identified a skill development need and wish to collaborate with the teacher who is the best at this in your organization. While waiting for the necessary permissions, find what published authors have done to research and develop the skill.

Hopefully, you will soon be observing and working with an experienced practitioner but, if this 'official' approach fails, just ask around and approach individual teachers directly.

Recommended reading

Brookfield, S. (2009) The concept of critical reflection: promises and contradictions, *European Journal of Social Work*, 12(3): 293–304.

Brown, J. and Smyth, W. (2010) *Improving Practice Through Collaborative Professional Learning*. Belfast: LSDA Northern Ireland, www.lsdani.org.uk (accessed 3 May 2011).

Freire, P. (1992) *Pedagogy of Hope*. London: Continuum.

Trifonas, P.P. (2009) Deconstructing research: paradigms lost, *International Journal of Research and Methods in Education*, 32(3): 297–308.

www.oursubject.hud.ac.uk (free of charge to join)

5

Guided reflective practice

The chapter on collaborating in reflective practice with colleagues has established that reflection is not necessarily a solitary pursuit. This chapter will explore ways of working with tutors on teacher education courses and mentors in the professional situation to benefit from their advice and guidance on practice. We will start by considering building an effective relationship with the tutor to receive guidance on *how* to reflect and *what* to reflect on. Then we turn to the relationship with the mentor in the teaching and learning environment and in particular guidance in reflecting on 'subject specialism'.

The teacher education tutor

The role of the teacher education tutor is to enable the trainee teacher to develop both knowledge and understanding of teaching and learning and the ability to teach in the LLS. Most teacher education courses, whatever their level and duration, incorporate reflection on learning and practice. It is likely then that the tutor will encourage, and indeed in many cases require, trainee teachers to reflect. The tutor then will often be concerned not only with; *what* trainees reflect upon, but also *how* they reflect. The student teacher is likely to be introduced to a basic model of reflection that they can put to use right away. Depending on the level of the teacher education course the tutor may introduce the student teacher to more detailed models of reflection, for example Brookfield (1995). A seemingly obvious point, but one nonetheless worth making, is that whatever the model the student is introduced to, it is important that they use it. The tutor will offer it not as an abstract element of knowledge but as a tool to be used in the professional practice of teaching. It may be that on some teacher education courses the choice of the model of reflection (within reason) is that of the students, but be that as it may, the tutor is likely to require evidence of an *engagement* with the process of reflection. In assessing a trainee's engagement, the tutor may comment on *how* they are reflecting, that is to say not only on the topic or issue being reflected upon, but the level or depth of reflection. These comments are useful because they are a guide to the student on whether reflections are too 'descriptive'. This is common in trainees who are reflecting on learning and practice for the first time. Guidance from a tutor can help the trainee teacher explore not only the 'what' but also the 'why'. Of course the tutor can only do this if the trainee is fully engaged with the process of reflection. It is important therefore that the trainee 'practises' reflection, for instance by ensuring that the reflective journal (if it is a requirement of the teacher education course) is kept up to date and that the trainee's own teaching sessions are reflected upon on a regular basis.

The other element of guidance on reflection offered by the teacher education tutor is on the content, *what* is to be reflected upon. This can be divided into two, the first is *abilities* and the second is *knowledge and understanding*. Abilities include the planning of learning, the use of teaching and learning methods, using teaching resources, the production and use of learning materials, communicating with the learner, differentiation of learning and group management skills. Knowledge and understanding include that of theories of learning, government policy relating to the LLS and 'good practice'. Teacher education tutors will be quick to point out that these two elements should not be regarded as being isolated from each other. It is important to see teaching and learning in the classroom or workshop as being *informed* by theories and exemplars of good practice, something we will return to later.

Planning of learning

If we consider the planning of learning, this will be the production of planning documentation such as schemes of work and session plans, topic selection, timings of teaching and learning activities, the sequencing of learning, the preparation of the learning environment and the planning to meet individual learning needs. The tutor may offer guidance on the structure and the content of the planning documentation. Trainee teachers will of course be given exemplars of session plans and schemes of work, but these need to be 'tailored' to suit the actual professional situation of the trainee teacher. Tutors' comments on what information needs to be included in planning documentation, and how those documents should be presented, help the trainee teacher tailor exemplar documentation to the actual professional situation, particularly important where the trainee is teaching in an organization that does not have planning templates. In these cases the tutor's comments will help the trainee teacher to reflect upon what information needs to be included on documents such as schemes of work and session plans. The ability to select *what* is to be taught and *when* is an important one in the planning of learning. The tutor will be able to offer guidance on how to relate the content of schemes of work, training plans and session plans to course specifications or training needs analyses, to ensure that aims and objectives for the learning are clearly identified. Once what is to be taught is identified, the teacher needs to give consideration to the time allotted to the learning activities and how these activities are sequenced, both across a course or module and within a session. A teacher education tutor will be able to offer guidance on whether too much or too little time has been planned for a learning activity, enabling the student teacher to reflect and make the necessary changes for when that learning activity is used again. An example is where the student teacher plans to use small group work as an activity; quite often too little time is allotted for feedback and discussion, meaning that some of the value of the activity is lost. In verbal and written feedback to the student teacher the tutor may comment about the time allotted to encourage changes to be made. Similarly with the sequencing of learning, the teacher education tutor may have comment to make on how the student teacher has planned for one activity to go before or after another which can be reflected upon and changes made to sequencing of learning activities in the future. Another aspect of professional practice that student teachers often find challenging is the planning to meet individual learning needs. In many situations the teacher needs to *differentiate* learning, for example by content where there is more than one level of attainment in the group. The tutor's comments on how this differentiation is planned and executed will help the student teacher reflect upon whether enough challenge is being offered to the 'higher' level or more able learners and whether enough support is being offered to the 'lower' level or less able learners. Guidance may also be given on how the needs of learners with a disability are being met, for instance those who have dyslexia. Tutor's comments on how well learning resources are deployed and learning materials adapted to meet those needs can help the student teacher reflect upon practice in this area and extend their repertoire of skills.

Teaching and learning methods

In observing the professional practice of the student teacher, the teacher education tutor is able to comment on the appropriateness of the methods employed and how well they are used. Most teachers will use 'exposition' or whole group teaching in their practice. The tutor's comments on its use will enable the student teacher to reflect on its use: is it being used too much? Is it being used at the right time in a session? Are there opportunities for learners to ask questions for clarification? Does the teacher 'keep to the point? Are new or technical words and terms explained to the group? For those teachers who teach 'vocational' subjects such as hairdressing, brickwork and motor vehicle mechanics, the use of demonstrations is an important part of the repertoire of teaching skills. The tutor will be able to offer comment how well a procedure or skill is communicated to learners, once more inviting the student teacher to consider whether the teaching method *involves* the learner, perhaps through participation or question and answer. The teacher education tutor may well leave the responsibility for feedback on the 'technical' aspects of a demonstration, for example the use of specialist tools, to the student teacher's mentor, unless of course the tutor shares the same subject specialism as the student teacher.

It is widely acknowledged it is important for learners to be 'active' in their learning (see Petty 2004; Duckett and Tatarkowsky 2005) therefore it is important that the student teacher reflect upon the selection and use of learning activities to promote that active learning. The teacher education tutor will offer comments that should inform the reflections of the student teacher. These comments are likely to include those on the appropriateness of the learning method being used. Is it the right method to meet the objectives of a particular session? The teacher education tutor will be alert in an observation to point out where learning activities are being included merely to get the learners 'active'; tutors' comments on appropriateness can guide the student teacher in reflecting on how a learning activity 'fits' with the rest of the session to help meet the objectives. Tutor feedback on the management of learning activities can help the student teacher consider ways to make the learning experience more effective. Comment on timings of the activity can help the student teacher reflect upon the amount of time needed, and whether the activity is positioned at the 'right' time in a session. The student teacher may seek guidance on how the discussion and feedback after a learning activity such as small group work is managed to gain maximum benefit from it for the learners.

Teaching and learning resources and materials

There is a wide range of teaching and learning resources available to the teacher in most professional settings. The ability to select and use those resources is an important one for student teachers to develop. In the observation of teaching the tutor may comment on the appropriateness of the resource used. PowerPoint presentations for instance using a data projector and electronic board are a staple in the teacher's repertoire, but overuse can induce tedium in the learner. DVDs can be a valuable way of introducing visual representation but tend to date quickly. Comment from the teacher education tutor can help the student teacher consider the balance of using such resources, weighing up the advantages and the disadvantages.

Most teachers are likely to distribute learning materials to their learners, both electronic and paper based. Increasing use is being made of virtual learning environments or platforms (VLE/VLP) to make learning materials available to the learner which can be accessed outside class time. It may be that during a teaching observation a tutor may not necessarily see the VLE/VLP being used, so it may be a good idea for the student teacher to make a special arrangement for the tutor to see the learning materials placed there. Comment could be invited not only on the quality of the learning materials themselves, but also the learner access to them.

During a teaching observation the tutor is often required to give feedback to the student teacher on paper based learning materials. These can include handouts, worksheets, work books and handouts. Comment can be made on two aspects of the learning materials. First, the production of the materials, the quality of reproduction and legibility for instance. Second, there is the use the materials by the learner – are they readily understood by the learners for whom they are designed? Do they promote active learning? And do they take account of individual learning needs, for instance those of the dyslexic learner?

Communication with the learner

This is an area of professional practice where the student teacher can gain valuable feedback from the teacher education tutor after a teaching observation. The tutor may comment on verbal communication, including audibility and clarity of delivery, the language used and the tone of voice. Another important aspect of verbal communication is the teacher's use of question and answer technique. Feedback is likely to include that on the types of questions asked, whether they were 'closed' or 'open', the level of the questioning, whether it offered enough challenge for the learner or whether it was too difficult, and the purpose of the questioning – was it a recap of previous learning or was it designed to 'build' understanding through the use of scaffolding questions or to assess learner knowledge and understanding? Other aspects of communication include eye contact with the learners and the use of gestures. During a teaching observation the tutor will be able to assess whether the teacher is able to maintain eye contact with the learners, either during whole group teaching or small group work. The tutor can also look out for any gestures and mannerisms that might distract the learners. There is an increasing use of recording of student teachers' practice in teacher education, which enables the tutor to point out clearly areas for development. This is of course a valuable source of reflection for the student teacher.

Group management skills

This is an aspect of professional practice which seems to cause particular anxiety in the new teacher – what happens if they do not do what I tell them?

There is of course more to group management than the behavioural issues, but nonetheless it is something on which that the student teacher is likely to seek guidance (or reassurance!). There are various techniques on managing learner behaviour that the tutor may suggest, but – and this highlights the importance of reflection – the student teacher has to use those techniques in their own situation; there are rarely 'off-the-peg' solutions in teaching and learning. After a teaching observation the tutor may offer comment on aspects of group management such as seating arrangements and facilitating small group work, i.e. managing the learning environment to ensure effective learning.

Integrating 'published knowledge' and practice

The teacher education tutor has a crucial role in enabling the student teacher to integrate what Usher and Edward (1994) call 'published knowledge' with the practice of teaching. Published knowledge includes theories of learning but also elements of 'good practice' and government policy and legislation on the wider FE sector.

Most teacher education courses require the student teacher to have some knowledge of learning theories, but importantly this is not meant to be an 'abstract' knowledge; often student teachers have to demonstrate how theory 'underpins' or 'informs' their practice. The teacher education tutor is likely to outline the theories that they feel are relevant, with the student teacher reflecting on what has been taught, supplemented of course by reading recommended texts. The reflection on what has been learned, putting it in the context of one's own professional situation, is the key to the integration of that knowledge with practice.

Government policy and legislation on the wider FE sector has of course had an impact on the role of the teacher and is therefore likely to be part of the syllabus on a teacher education course. However the sector is diverse, and not all that information will be relevant to every student teacher '14 to 19'. It is up to the student teacher to consider the policy and legislation that is relevant to their professional situation and to reflect upon how it influences professional practice.

How does the student teacher make the most of the opportunities to enlist the help of the tutor in integrating published knowledge and practice? The first way is for them to read the course documentation carefully – what are the requirements to integrate knowledge and practice? Does the course require a knowledge of learning theories, if so how many? This kind of preparation helps the student teacher organize their own study and demonstrates to the tutor a willingness to engage with the course.

Second the student teacher should read the texts recommended by the tutor; it is not enough to rely on notes from classes. This seems an obvious point, but concerns are often raised among teacher educators that many student teachers do not do the reading necessary to form a basis for integration of knowledge and practice. Third the student teacher should ask questions of the tutor, either in class or tutorials. These questions can clarify whether a certain learning theory is relevant to the student teacher's practice, but of course also where a student has difficulty understanding policy or theory. The tutor often has very limited time for tutorials, so it is helpful if the student teacher has their questions prepared beforehand where possible. The relationship between the reflective student teacher and the teacher education tutor is not a passive one. It is not a matter of waiting to be 'told what to do', but rather the student teacher being prepared, through reading and reflection on practice, for the meetings with the teacher education tutor, either in class or the tutorial.

The mentor

The mentor has an important part to play in the student teacher's reflective practice for two interrelated reasons. First the mentor is the person the teacher has contact with on a regular basis in the professional situation, either a placement in the case of 'pre-service' student teachers, or employing institution in that of the 'in-service' student teachers. Second the mentor has the same 'subject specialism' as the student teacher. Greater emphasis has been placed on professional development in teachers' subject specialisms in recent years in the policy on teacher training and development in the LLS (see Burton et al. 2010). The mentor has a pivotal role in guiding the reflections of the student teacher on aspects of organization in the professional situation and also the practice of teaching a particular subject.

Organization

The mentor is usually an experienced person, not only in their teaching, but also where the organization is concerned, so they will 'know their way around' and will thus be a valuable guide to the student teacher. For the student on placement in the education and training organization the mentor will often be the first point of contact, welcoming them and responsible for the 'orientation' to the organization. Here the mentor is literally a 'guide', directing the student teacher to classrooms or workshops, the photocopier and hopefully somewhere to sit in the staffroom! The student teacher who is well prepared can turn these aspects of the relationship with the mentor into an opportunity for reflection by asking questions of the mentor of the 'how' and 'why' variety.

Case study

Tabitha is a student on a Pre-Service Certificate in Education course who is starting her worked based experience (WBE) at a FE college. She has been met by her mentor at the reception area and has been taken on a tour of the college and its facilities. She is shown the busy print room and how to fill out a requisition for the printing of learning materials. Tabitha has the presence of mind to ask how long she would have to wait between the requisition and receiving the printed materials. The mentor informs her that the minimum time would be three working days and the maximum six working days. He goes on to say that it is likely to be at the maximum end because it is early in the academic year and there is a great demand for the printing of course materials.

Later in the staff room the mentor apprises Tabitha of the college and departmental policies that she needs to be aware of. He tells her that the teachers in the department are rigorous in maintaining the policy on learner lateness to sessions. Tabitha is told that if a learner is later than ten minutes to a session without authorization from the course tutor she not to allow them in. She asks her mentor why there is this strict adherence in the department and is told that are two reasons, first there had been problems with some learners coming into the sessions up to half an hour late and therefore disrupting learning activities, and second as the department was teaching vocational courses it was felt that learners should be prepared for the world of work, which includes punctuality.

By asking her questions of the tutor Tabitha has given herself the material to reflect on how a college functions and why.

Teaching a specialist subject

There are two aspects of teaching a specialist subject that a student teacher might seek guidance from a mentor. First there is the body of subject knowledge itself and second the teaching and learning methods, activities, resources and materials necessary for teaching that subject specialism.

The guidance sought from the mentor on subject knowledge will of course depend in large part on the nature of the subject specialism. Discussions between a student psychology teacher and the mentor are likely in part at least to be about the theories that have to be taught and learned. For the student teacher and mentor teaching electrical installation the discussion will include not only theory, but the regulations current in the industry. However all student teachers are likely to seek guidance on the actual course requirements for subject specialist knowledge. Those new to teaching may have a level of subject knowledge many times higher than their learners. The mentor can give guidance on what in the student teacher's body of knowledge is appropriate to impart to the learners; this guidance will help the student reflect on the 'levelness' of the learner where subject knowledge is concerned. Currency of subject knowledge may be another issue. Discussion between the mentor and student teacher will ascertain whether there is a requirement to introduce a new theory or regulation to the learners.

Practical activity

Consider your subject specialism. What aspects of subject knowledge would you need to discuss with your mentor?

The *ensemble* of teaching and learning methods, activities, resources and materials used by the teacher in the wider FE sector will depend in part on the subject specialism. Where teaching methods are concerned, the choice of the right one and its correct use are crucial for effective learning in a specialist subject. In the teaching and learning of plastering for example, 'demonstration' is an important teaching method. The teacher demonstrates a plastering technique to the learners before they practise it. Of course the quality of the demonstration will have an effect on the subsequent learning, so the student teacher seeks guidance from the mentor, probably by observing a demonstration by the mentor and reflecting later on what is necessary for a sound demonstration of plastering skills.

The student teacher has to develop the skills of selection and management of learning activities appropriate for the subject specialism. In the teaching of business studies, simulations are often used to allow the learner to experience what it is like to engage in business activities such as marketing, purchasing and selling. The student teacher may seek guidance from the mentor at the planning stage and also ask that the use of a simulation be observed by the mentor.

Some subject specialisms will have resources and materials which are peculiar to them, and where it will be necessary to seek guidance from a mentor. The use of textiles is crucial to the teaching and learning of fashion design, for example. Here the issue may be for the student teacher to assess how much material can be used by a group at any one time. It is only through discussion with a mentor that the teacher would be able to make that judgement. Where the use of certain resources is concerned, health and safety may be an important issue for the student teacher to consider. If electrical installation is once more taken as an example, observation of the mentor teaching in the workshop and subsequent discussion will help the student teacher to reflect on the importance of ensuring safe working practices.

Building an effective relationship with the mentor

How does the reflective student teacher get the best out of the relationship with the mentor? First by acknowledging that mentors are busy people; it is likely that they will have full teaching timetables and associated responsibilities. It is important that the student teacher is well prepared for meetings with the mentor, preferably by framing the questions they wish to ask; in this way best use is made of the often limited time available. Second the student teacher should be open to advice and guidance, and be prepared to act on the suggestions made by the mentor by reflecting on discussion and observations and changing practice as a consequence.

6

Extending reflective practice: action research

Teachers in our sector do not tend to see themselves as researchers, primarily because of what the sector and professional identities have become as a product of New Labour's seemingly constant reorganization of the sector (Avis 1999). Here, their legacy that is the overarching professional standards (LLUK 2005) can be seen as a grand narrative of performativity through prescribed and McDonaldized (Ritzer 1998) competences, which sit easily with Brown et al.'s (2008) notion of professional Taylorism where permission to think is denied teachers. In other words, New Labour's teacher is not supposed to be a researcher since there are other, more important, boxes to tick in the working day. Hopkins (2002) argues that we (teachers, students and society) deserve something better.

As we suggested in Chapter 1 the purpose of reflective practice, and also of action research into one's own context, lies at the heart of the teacher's role. Hopkins, working with the emancipatory work of Stenhouse (1975), justifies this purpose as:

> The major consequence of doing this is that teachers take more control of their professional lives. Not content to be told what to do or being uncertain about what one is doing, teachers who engage in their own research are developing their professional judgement and are moving towards emancipation and autonomy.
>
> (Hopkins 2002: 32–3)

Sadly, action research seems to have begun snapping at the heels of reflective practice by becoming the next educational concept to become in danger of being over-theorized. From Ebbutt's (1985) stance that action research is not true research unless it has been published and opened to scrutiny by fellow professionals, to Somekh's (2006) centrality of eight methodological principles, action research has come a long way since Lewin (1946) first introduced it as a vehicle for social enquiry. Thus, there is a rich vein of literature for those pursuing higher degrees although here we are simply concerned with action research as has been usefully defined by Hopkins (2002: 1): 'My vision is of teachers who have extended their role to include critical reflection upon their craft with the aim of improving it.' Dewey, who we met in Chapter 2, firmly located such an ethos alongside reflective practice rather earlier when he stated (1933:

83) 'The mind at every stage of growth has its own logic. It entertains suggestions, tests them by observation of objects and events, reaches conclusions, tries them in action, finds them confirmed or in need of correction or rejection.' Consequently, and after much deliberation, we offer the notion that educational action research goes beyond reflective practice by embracing these key features:

- a planned enquiry into teaching and learning in the practitioner's own context and subject specialism;
- that such generated knowledge is shared with critically reflective members of a community of enquiry;
- that such enquiry should count as a form of professional development for the practitioner.

Amid the plethora of theories relating to action research there are two approaches worth bringing to the reader's attention: those of the internalized and externalized approaches. Quite simply, the externalized approach relies on the interpretation of action, as perceived by observers, in relation to a value base set by others. One example of this is where a peer or trusted colleague observes a session, according to Ofsted criteria, then re-observes the session after improvements have been made. The externalized approach (Kemmis and McTaggart 1981) is deeply contested, since it seems to place a higher value on theory than on practice, although it lends itself to accommodating the multiple agencies who have a stake in the post-14 classroom. In contrast, the internalized approach is personal and individualized. McNiff (1993: 16) describes it as: 'An I-(internalised) enquiry is that conducted by the individual into her own practice. She reflects critically on her work, either privately or in discussion with others, and aims to think of original ways that will help her improve. The status of an I-enquiry is personal.' Indeed, McNiff advances an unashamed passionate advocacy for the personalized nature of action research where own values, ethics and self-development need to be clearly understood and rationalized before development of learners can be facilitated.

This sort of enquiry or 'insider research', while originating in the personal context, lends itself to the sharing of findings with colleagues and other interested parties within the practitioner's community of practice. Here, teachers know 'what works' in their own sessions and with particular types of learners although they tend not to have much of an enquiring nature regarding the equally good practice that goes on in other teachers' sessions, hence our suggestion that findings and best practice should be shared. Consequently, when as teachers we discover what works there is little incentive to pursue improvement further, yet this, we suggest, is the hallmark of the true professional and is our justification of why action research enquiries should be credited as CPD.

It is worth mentioning that an action research enquiry does not need to start from a problem although it must have a focus on improving some aspect of teaching and/ or learning within the practitioner's context. To illustrate the difference, the first case study in this chapter adopts an internal approach to resolving a problem while the second leans more towards the externalized approach in seeking to improve teaching and learning as a strategic endeavour.

Case study 1: the life support machine

Sal teaches Personal, Social, Health and Citizenship Education (PSHCE) to foundation learning tier (FLT) students across a range of core programme areas for a private training organization that works in partnership with the local education authority and the local FE college. Students on the programme tend to be disadvantaged in some way and are drawn mostly from the pupil referral service (PRS), Year 11 pupils who are at risk of exclusion from compulsory schooling and those pursuing entry level awards in FE. Sal generally finds most of the students difficult since they tend to have short concentration spans, little motivation to learn and often present challenging behaviours to their teachers, one of the most prominent being their preoccupation with their mobile phones, which seem to assume the status of a life support machine for some students. Better behaved students tend to be quickly and inexorably drawn into challenging behaviour despite their potential to rise above it, a feature that Sal suspects is characteristic of either the programme or the culture of the learning environment.

Sal had spent a torrid first term working hard to separate many students from their phones during lessons but without success. It is an organizational policy that students are not allowed to use their mobile phones during lessons and she had exhausted all the sanctions in place without making any difference to the students' practice of seemingly texting under the desk. Enquiries among her colleagues suggested that the problem was widespread throughout the organization and defied all attempts to remedy it. Yet she was determined to turn the problem on its head and intended to try new, deliberate and even radical approaches in the following term. Before the Christmas break, during which Sal would be preparing for the new term where the focus of PSHCE would be on sex education, she discussed her plan with her manager, Dawn, in order to gain ethical and institutional clearance that legitimated her intention. The plan she outlined was, on the face of it, quite simple but loaded with tension, the rationale being as follows:

- Many students would be receiving new, latest generation mobile phones as Christmas presents and the novelty value could make them inseparable in January; thus, there was potential for the problem to be worse than ever.
- Too much learning time is lost in addressing the use of phones.
- None of the sanctions appear to have any effect on students other than to aggravate behaviours when a phone is confiscated.

Sal's plan was that students would be required to use their mobile phones as learning resources, but only in the one-hour PSHCE sessions and with one experimental group, as a pilot for a trial period of six weeks whereupon the trial would be evaluated by Sal and Dawn. To assist in the evaluation, Sal would be required to maintain a reflective diary chronicling the successes, weaknesses and tensions of the pilot. At the end of term staff briefing as an item of any other business, Dawn outlined the purpose and method of the research that would be a feature of one of Sal's groups over the following half term and explained that the key findings of the research would be disseminated to the teaching team at its conclusion. Sal's reflective diary is reproduced here:

Session 1: 'peer pressure'

I shared the aims of the pilot study with the FLT Childcare group of 12 girls emphasizing that it was only for six weeks, applied to no other groups and that institutional ground rules still applied to other subject areas and sessions that they attended. I offered, in the interests of equality, that I-touch devices were available (on a six-week loan from the ICT department) for any learners who did not have an I-phone. There was a distinct buzz from the group as they carried out the first task of exchanging mobile phone numbers with each other. Here, I wanted to establish not so much a community of practice but a community network since I wanted to embrace whatever sense of culture they shared. I also wanted to cede responsibility to the more challenging learners, my rationale being that the most difficult might respond well to taking turns each week to be the 'coordinator'. The coordinator would be nominated by me at the start of each session (Jane this week) and it would be her job to collate responses from the others and to transfer them to either the wipe board or flip chart.

I asked the group for a list of people whose opinions they value to be sent to Jane by text who would then write them on the board. When Jane started populating the board I realized that one of the roles of the coordinator should be to transcribe the messages from text-speak to correct language – my first mistake, and this procedure took five minutes longer than anticipated. As a group we explored key themes from the communal list, one of which was that they implied that they only take notice of people who see them in a positive or complementary light. We developed their material into issues of peer pressure, through whole group discussion, without any distractions. Here, I noticed that we moved forward much more quickly since there were no interruptions and the girls gave a distinct impression of being satisfied simply by 'promenading' their phones on the desk. I was left at the end of the session pondering whether, normally, they send texts or just simply 'mess' with their phones since I didn't notice any incoming texts or see any of them using the keys.

Session 2: 'relationships'

I started by recapping the previous session by having the girls text the key learning points to Sue, the coordinator for this week, who read them aloud. I gave the students five minutes to each find one example of how relationships are portrayed in the media with the intention of sharing them and discussing whether they reflect the reality of our lives, then numbering them and ranking them according to their accuracy before breaking into three groups of four to discuss them.

Once Sue had received all the examples of relationships she suggested that they could be 'Blue-Toothed' to the Smart board (this was immediately beyond me) and they were suddenly all there for the whole group to see (much more effective than reading them out or describing them). I had anticipated that they would look for advertisements on the internet but most of the contributions were short video clips, with personal tweeted messages coming a close second, from social network sites. The tweets were amazing and gave a clear sense of cultural disposition that I was not expecting where a wide age range were quite open, even graphic, about their relationships and emotions. Several of these provoked debate in ways that I could not have hoped for beforehand and the key points seemed to emerge quite easily. Since I was more of a spectator at this point I wrote what I thought were the emerging key issues and points on the flip chart while the girls got on with it. The hour seemed to fly and I had to interrupt the debate in order to consolidate the session.

I think that there were several key learning points for me in this session. Firstly, there is a particular youth culture that the girls relate to, if not co-exist within, that those outside their immediate age range are not privy to. Yet they also engage with the relationships of people twice their age and I thought that this was an interesting use of media on their own terms. Equally interesting, I suspect that five minutes was too short a time for them to surf the internet and instead they went straight to social networks that made readily available the type of material we were after – again, they seem to have techniques and methods that they immediately differentiate from. Secondly, and in a similar vein, the students have a much better idea than me of the types of resources that can be captured as learning aids and I have started to think that there is a certain richness in their culture that we teachers have completely ignored because we know better, yet it seems we don't. Thirdly, while the debates were heated, there was no texting and I had little to do other than make notes – they simply took control of the learning and achieved that which would have normally worn me out in achieving much less.

In contrast to my own steep learning curve there is also an element of the unknown which seems to grow each time they find what they are looking for. Here, I am mindful of not just the youth culture that I have been given a glimpse of but a technological culture which I sought to release on my own terms, but which has a greater potential when ownership of the enquiry and learning is relinquished to the learners. Yet I have a nagging concern that I may be releasing a beast from a cage that I may be unable to put back at half term.

Session 3: 'conception'

I planned this session so many times and in so many different ways that it almost wore me out over Christmas – and I was not confident in any of them. In the end I had three alternative session plans, extension activities and some rather tame resources from a previous era, but reflecting on my experience of the last two sessions I realized that there was something else going on with this group. Firstly, the need to embrace mobile phones in the sessions seems to have become a secondary issue. Secondly, I need to trust the learners to take control of their own learning – which is what they clearly do the moment I let go. Thirdly, the learning needs to be located within their own culture and context – which I know little about despite my previous efforts to have them believe that I am street-wise and one of their equals. Finally, I had to accept that a radical approach to managing this group had to strike a balance between risk-taking, on my part, and the integrity of the firewall.

I started the session by having the students tell me the key learning outcomes from the previous session, the objectives of this session and appointing Nasreen as coordinator. My thinking at this point was that Nasreen's cultural identity and forceful nature might make her an effective censor where no firewall exists between the mobile phones and the Smart board, I imagine.

I paired the students and gave them 10 minutes to find an animated portrayal of human conception while both stating and writing on the board that practical demonstrations, reconstructions and rehearsals involving real people were strictly forbidden. I was amazed at both how quickly they found them and what 'the system' allowed through although Nasreen did an excellent job of vetting them on each 'phone before Blue-Toothing them to the Smart board. None of the students thought the material to be a revelation, regardless of ethnic or cultural origin, and said that they had explored the topic on the Childcare programme, although they continued to be baffled by the medical terminology and its pronunciation. Given that there was suddenly no need to pursue the topic of conception for a further 30 minutes, I got them to produce a poster of the key terminology with their own phonetic suggestions of how the words should be pronounced although there was noticeably more tinkering with phones at this point than in the previous sessions.

On reflection, I need not have worried about the session but I am mindful that it was a somewhat wasted hour which caused the girls, probably through the tedium of revisiting established knowledge, to revert to playing with their phones. Nevertheless, I am pleased that we developed phonetic skills and broadened vocabulary, that Nasreen seemed to come out of herself when given the opportunity and that the students seem much more natural and relaxed (although I'm not convinced that I'm reading them in a particularly reliable way). I think that I need to raise the bar, both for myself and the students, in order to better embrace the potential of phones and to relinquish more of the learning to them. I doubt that this is what Dawn had in mind when she consented to this pilot but I need tangible proof that what I'm trying to do is having an impact on learning.

Session 4: 'STIs'

I started the session by displaying the poster from the previous week and having the students take turns to pronounce the terminology before outlining the objectives of the session and issuing sick bags. The students were paired differently to the previous session and each pair picked a card at random from:

- Chlamydia
- Gonorrhoea
- Non-specific urethritis
- Trichomonas vaginalis
- Genital warts
- Syphilis
- Genital herpes

The task was to research the cause, symptoms and treatment of the chosen sexually transmitted infection (STI) and to produce a photograph that could be used as part of a one-minute presentation to their peers (I had photographs available in case they couldn't find any). I gave the group 10 minutes to find the information from their phones, 10 minutes to make sense of it and 10 minutes to produce a presentation with an overall 10 minutes for the presentations with turn-rounds. The slowest pair had the information within three minutes and the research came together in the intended way with an uncharacteristic level of vigour, apparent disgust and some laughter. I have no idea why they found any of this funny. I hadn't intended the task to be competitive but there was a distinct atmosphere of each pair wanting to produce something that surpassed the others' presentations and I thought it might be useful to see what they could arrive at when clearly focused and driven as they apparently were. Once the first pair sent the photo and information to their college ICT storage area the others followed suit with some splendid results being achieved through a photo enhancing package and then incorporated into a PowerPoint presentation. I was suddenly grateful that I did not need to show my pre-prepared photos which waned in comparison to the quality achieved by the girls.

The presentations, accompanied by plenty of predictable 'Yuk' noises, were excellent in terms of content while the ad-hoc description by each pair tended to be good and amounted to reading the PowerPoint text to their audience. Yet these are young girls who do not normally engage in directed learning, shrink back from speaking aloud and seem to bear the hallmarks of those who have been fed an unrequited diet of, 'You are a failure', thus far. Nula coordinated the presentations and ensured that we gave each presentation a round of applause and they easily located the risk of casual relationships with the possible risk of STIs. I heaped praise on the group for their efforts as part of the conclusion but some of them seemed uncomfortable with this.

Notwithstanding the many plus points of this session, I was left with the distinct feeling that I had left them with very good knowledge of one STI but only a mere dusting of the other five – something like 16% competent in STI knowledge. How do I ensure that such really good and reliable learning outcomes are shared by all the students? Put it on the VLE? Can this be captured as evidence for assessment? It seems that the more we pilot this study the more questions it raises – will be good to hear what the others teachers suggest for this.

Session 5: 'contraception'

I have always felt this topic to be the most embarrassing, especially for me, and have worked tirelessly to find ways in which the subject can be learnt in a mature and adult way. Following our Ofsted inspection last year when I was given a grade 2 for this session, I have ceased to try to improve on what I currently do since my stock lesson obviously passes muster. However, I realize that I can't abandon the phone pilot and have been encouraged by the previous sessions to give the learners a free rein while keeping the stock lesson plan and materials as back-up if it goes wrong.

The introduction to the session confirmed that the learners remembered precious little of the others' chosen STIs and the presenters (I called them 'experts') were quick to clarify whenever something incorrect was offered or a key point missed entirely. Lasting 15 minutes, this took much longer than my customary five-minute 'splash-and-go' recap but I thought that it was a particularly effective form of social learning where they learn much from each other rather than from me. The main activity was not unlike the previous session where, in yet different pairs, they chose a form of contraception from the following:

- Dutch cap
- Coil
- Condom
- Spermicide
- Copper intrauterine
- Contraceptive patch
- Birth control pill

The task was to research the method of contraception, list the advantages and disadvantages, state the efficiency of the method in percentage terms and produce a presentation to their peers, including a visual representation if appropriate, in a form that their peers could take away with them electronically. I had no idea what this electronic form might be but trusted that the students would come up with something. The results were similar to the previous session in terms of learner engagement, the quality of produced work and the competitive undercurrent in the session.

Yet there were three clear differences in comparison. Firstly, Dawn arrived as I was part way through the introduction of the task and stayed until the end. The learners didn't notice her at first but I was deeply embarrassed, mainly at my foolhardy approach to relinquishing control of the learning, not having any idea of how they might share their findings and setting up the students to look foolish in front of her during their presentations. Secondly, there was a clear shift in their confidence levels when they made their presentations and I can only guess that this was because they had an idea of what to expect and that they may have reflected on their previous session's presentations. Thirdly, they suggested a range of mechanisms by which the presentations could be shared with peers through what sounded like a toolkit of 'Apps', Blue Tooth, email, 'drop box' and something else that I can't remember. As all eyes were fixed on me for an answer, including Dawn's, I suggested that Dani (the coordinator for the session) should decide on a method whereby they all immediately receive others' presentation work and she opted for Blue Tooth. I concluded the session in much the same way as the previous week while praying for the ground to open beneath me.

She floored me with her opening remark of, 'Where did you learn all that technological stuff?' to which I replied, 'From the girls'. 'In four hours while teaching them? Are you serious?' I felt instantly vindicated. In all, Dawn believed that we were onto something, not just in terms of the girls' behaviour but their level of engagement, the ease with which they collaborated during their work and their readiness to make decisions for themselves.

Session 6: 'myths and facts'

The introduction to the session revealed that the learners retained much more of their peers' presentations from the previous week despite none of them admitting that they had since looked at the received work. I didn't understand this but pressed ahead with what I hoped would be a light-hearted session to conclude the pilot where the students would research a given belief, make a judgement of whether it was a myth or a fact and pose it to the rest of the group where it would be voted on with laminated True/ False cards.

Whilst the learners had previously worked well in pairs to complete a task, I decided to focus on individual tasks in order to broaden the range of enquiry. This turned out to be a mistake since they were no longer learning with each other and there were a number of phone and other distractions as a result. I informed the group that once they had completed their individual task they were to compare and contrast their findings with a peer of their own choice and to pose the two beliefs or statements as a pair to the rest of the group, a move that coincided with the end of the distractions. The power of collaboration and peer learning never ceases to amaze me.

It seemed to have taken me a long time to draw up 12 myths or facts but they worked well to invigorate discussion when paired and half of the pairs also concocted their own myths – again, I realized that I could have prepared one myth or fact for each group and asked them to devise one or two others since they enjoyed doing this.

There was plenty of laughter and cries of, 'Prove it! No way!' etc. during the plenary. Tonya suggested that we could use the Interactive Voting Pads that they use on TV for audience participation but I hadn't thought of that. (They're in a cupboard somewhere but no one uses them because it apparently takes ages to input the questions beforehand). I imagine that the coordinator could probably manage this as part of her role, or use the stopwatch on a phone to time the voting, next time I do this session.

Conclusion

Sal and Dawn spent time critically exploring the journal with Dawn questioning many of Sal's comments and both clearly saw the benefits of the research but were mindful of the potential difficulties, for example, students using their own phone credit, the power of peer pressure for everyone to have the latest phone and the potential for learners to openly text without engaging with the learning. Sal felt that she had been both lucky yet deeply blessed during the pilot and both agreed that she should repeat the pilot during the next half term with a different group, on a different subject, while embedding what she had learnt from the initial pilot. At the staff briefing before the half term break, Sal gave a 10-minute overview of the outcomes of the study to her colleagues, noted their reluctance to accept her account of the improvements in behaviour and offered an open door policy to colleagues to observe during the next half term. At the end of summer term Inset day, Sal led a one-hour session on the use of mobile phones in the classroom where she modelled a range of innovative techniques with her colleagues.

Case study 2: blended learning and HE in FE

Steve teaches a first year part-time BA module 'Introduction to Research Methods' in an FE college. Following staff restructuring and the introduction of a blended learning approach to HE in FE, the college has merged core units from its range of BA programmes, validated by different HEIs but having strikingly similar module outcomes and assessment requirements, in order to maximize class sizes, reduce duplication and utilize the college VLE. As a result, Steve felt a certain uneasiness since a colleague in health and social care (H&SC) had been made redundant and her seven students have been timetabled for the module with his nine education studies (ES) students. Against another tension of having students outside his subject specialism, and having pondered over the changes long and hard over the summer break, Steve sees the situation as an opportunity to teach the module in a different way, to create a focus of enquiry into alternative pedagogies and to model the concept of action research to the undergraduates. He has two plans for this which he shares with the students at the first session.

The first plan is to build on the 'two letters' approach that had transformed his teaching since he read Cowan (1998: 52–3) ten years previously who suggested that at the end of an academic year the students should collaborate in the writing of two letters – one to the tutor advising him/her of how to improve the teaching and/or learning of the module learning outcomes; the other letter to next year's students advising them of how to maximize their study efforts and time on the programme. Steve had maintained this for each undergraduate year he taught using the tutor letter as part of his course evaluation, and to supplement the data from trends in grades, student satisfaction evaluations and moderation feedback from HEI partners, although he often found that students went off at a tangent and included advice about other modules and tutors. In amending his 'two letters' approach in recent years he had confined it to his modules, rather than the year, and had always issued the student letter, warts and all, to the next cohort at their induction. Steve legitimated the two letters as a form of externalized action research since the interpretations of teaching and learning, and their attendant value systems, were set by the learners. Over the years he found that such beliefs tended to shift, depending on the cultures and individual experiences and dispositions of the learners, yet the formula seemed to work well for him in developing the following year's curriculum and learner experience. As a firm advocate of students telling the teacher about their learning, successive cycles of his action research had seen him introduce bridging work as preparation for undergraduate study, support for academic writing and peer assessment of draft assignments, in addition to constantly developing the use of social and constructivist models of learning. This year, given that there was no 'student letter' concerning CFGs (critical friendship groups), he would be seeking weekly emails from students to update him on the progress of their learning.

The second plan was potentially much more troublesome. Steve had been mindful during his preparation for the module that he would need to legitimate the blended learning approach (which he defined as 'a student-centred approach combining taught, mixed method and distance-learning resources') to the group since they might raise thorny questions regarding what return they would be seeing from their tuition fees. Here, he did not have a letter from past students telling either him or a new learner what it would be like studying the module in two taught sessions instead of the traditional eight. The programme outline was designed as follows:

Week 1 (taught):	Module introduction
	Introduction to social research
	Formation of CFGs/Learning Sets
Week 2 (CFGs):	Planning a research project
	Hypothesis testing and sampling techniques
	Questionnaire design and issues on validity and reliability
Week 3 (CFGs):	Quantitative research methods and techniques
Week 4 (CFGs):	Qualitative research methods and techniques
Week 5 (taught):	Project proposal presentations
	'Shoot the teacher'
Week 6 (CFGs):	Quantitative data analysis and statistics
Week 7 (CFGs):	Qualitative data analysis and statistics
Week 8 (CFGs):	Critical review of case studies
	Peer review of draft project assignments
	Submit draft project assignment
	Module evaluation and 'two letters'
Week 12:	Final submission of project assignment

At the first taught session, following a five-minute 'getting to know you' icebreaker, Steve outlined his plans to the students where he intended to model learner-centred approaches in the first session that sought to persuade the students that they could achieve more on their own and with peers than through attending taught sessions for eight weeks. He then issued the module handbook for the separate programmes and set the following 10-minute individual task for the group:

> Interpret the module requirements for your programme.
> State what you need to do in order to achieve the module outcomes.
> Share your understanding with the person next to you.
> If there is any disparity between your understandings, clarify it with another pair.
> Once you have reached a common understanding share your thoughts with another small group.

Steve had used this 'snowball' approach many times before and found it to be an effective way of quickly reaching a consensus among a group, making the students work hard to arrive at the correct answers without lecturing or telling a group and that it gave him an opportunity to check the levels of understanding and engagement through eavesdropping on small group dialogue. He immediately noticed that students only worked with those from the same core programme, a feature that he had hoped to avoid.

The next task was for the learners to pair with someone they had not worked with in the previous task in completing the following activity:

Define the term 'social research'.
Suggest three reasons for conducting social research.
Suggest three qualities that a social researcher should possess.
Provide at least one academic source you have referred to in this task.
Be prepared to make a one-minute presentation of your findings to the rest of the group.
You have 20 minutes and the resources available on this site.

One pair went straight to the core text for the module which one of them had bought earlier; two pairs started by using their mobile phones to search the internet for answers; one pair used the classroom computer to access the internet; one pair picked through a pile of text books Steve had placed at the front of class but not mentioned and the remainder headed for the library on the next floor. The task took nearly 30 minutes but Steve was pleased with the results and gave plenty of praise and reward for their efforts.

For the next activity he paired them again, with one from each specialism, and asked each pair to produce a flip chart poster contrasting the advantages and disadvantages of critical friendship groups (CFGs) or learning sets (LSs), as they understood them, in five minutes. Pairs were then joined with other unfamiliar pairs to make quartets and given a journal abstract relating to CFGs with the following task:

Identify three key points from the abstract.
Distinguish features in the abstract that suggest your poster overview may give an incomplete account.
Describe the research method used by the author(s).
Modify your two posters and be prepared to explain your reasoning to the rest of the group.

The students seemed to struggle with this task and Steve realized, from the dialogue at each work station, that some of the H&SC group had never seen an abstract before. He concluded before the break by asking a list of direct questions he had prepared beforehand, and amended during the group tasks, then gave them their 'break task' (something he had introduced two years ago to maintain the evening's momentum through informal peer discussion):

Identify three peers who you would like to form a CFG/LS with for the module.
Suggest a preferred way of meeting together on a weekly basis (a room was booked for them in college and the HE study room in the library was available for booking).
Identify the person who is prepared to contact me weekly.

During break he re-arranged the room into four separate study areas, one for each CFG, each with its own laptop and Wi-Fi connection.

Following the break, he set them the next task in their CFGs:

> Negotiate the distribution of roles in order to complete the following task in 20 minutes:
>
> Select eight cards at random (each card stated a research-related term, e.g. ethnography, qualitative, sample, etc).
>
> Define the term.
>
> Reference the sources of each definition in Harvard format.
>
> Upload your terms, definitions and references into the module box on the VLE.
>
> Be prepared to make a one-minute presentation to the whole group of the process you went through.

Three of the groups appeared to be functioning well in a collaborative way while the fourth, comprising three students from H&SC and a lone ES student, seemed to be operating as a triplet with a spectator. Careful negotiation with consent from all concerned enabled a H&SC triplet and an ES quintet to be re-formed and the atmosphere and work ethic was immediately improved.

Steve brought the activity to a close through the four presentations then set the following 20-minute plenary activity in CFGs:

> Summarize the processes you have gone through in this session.
>
> Outline how those processes mirror social research.
>
> Evaluate how those processes contribute to CFGs.
>
> Describe how, where and when your CFG will meet and study.
>
> Synthesize the ways in which your CFG study will relate to your individual work for the module assignment.
>
> List any assistance you need from me.
>
> Be prepared to answer critical questions on the above from the other CFGs.

The plenary was something of a relief to Steve insofar as all groups seemed happy with the prospect of meeting and studying together in their own time while keeping in touch through a nominated CFG representative. Likewise, he was encouraged with their core learning from the session and the ways in which they were able to defend their perceptions regarding the first three questions.

Steve used a volunteer to navigate the module box on the VLE as a means of demonstrating where and how the weekly tasks and materials were accessed before discussing with them how the next three weeks' tasks could or should be managed in their groups. He concluded by giving an overview of what they needed to prepare for the taught session on week 5 when they would be giving a two-minute presentation to the wider group of what they intended their research plan to focus on. Here, there was a distinct advantage in the assessment requirements for the module on both programmes whereby students each needed to produce a research plan, but not one that needed to be carried out, and that draft submissions were promoted by both HEIs, and Steve wanted them to open their initial ideas to peer and tutor review before expending overtime on the plan.

At the second taught session on week 5, while sharing the objectives, Steve urged the group to reflect on the value of their CFGs and be prepared to share three thoughts before break:

Explain the key benefit of working in your CFG.
Outline how the CFG has contributed to your ideas for the project.
Suggest one way in which the CFG and/or blended learning approach could be improved for the remainder of the module.

The student presentations gave a sense of learners knowing the research questions they would pursue and the research paradigm that each would adopt. Steve was encouraged that the students were appropriately using research-oriented language found in the materials for the first four weeks and that they had a clear sense of how research can be used in their individual contexts, despite one or two being overly ambitious.

Following the presentation, Steve put the students back into their CFGs to answer the three questions on the flip chart and noticed a distinct contrast to how they had worked after break on the first week. Here, a natural leader had emerged in three of the groups (although the H&SC triplet seemed more collaborative), there was increased individual contribution and there was a fluency in the activity that he thought may have developed through familiarity with each other. While none of the answers to the first two questions surprised him, he was more interested in their thoughts regarding how the blended learning approach could be improved, and fixed if broken, midway through the module. Here, there was a clear sense that many students felt they were operating in silos and missing out on what the other groups were doing while a handful of students wanted clearer guidance on what they needed to do in order to achieve a 'first'.

Before sending them for break, Steve praised what they had produced by way of draft proposals, summarized their thoughts about blended learning and outlined what he meant by 'shoot the teacher', this being his version of a group tutorial where they could raise any issues of concern or clarification and which should form the basis of the 'break task' for this session.

During the break the room was re-arranged in a horseshoe of chairs with Steve in the centre. The tutorial activity produced no issues beyond those on the flip charts but heightened the learners' desire for exemplar materials, a predictable request that he had received in previous years and which formed the basis of the next activity, which did not appear on the programme outline since he did not want to 'lead' the group too much in their assignment work.

Once the groups were back in their CFGs Steve issued four fictitious assignments, based on the module outcomes, to each CFG and which he had produced over the summer: a H&SC quantitative research project (graded 72 per cent); a qualitative H&SC assignment (64 per cent); an ES quantitative project (62 per cent); and an ES qualitative piece (70 per cent). The task was:

Skim read the four assignments.
Identify three key features of each piece.
Suggest ways in which each 2.1 paper could be developed to break the grade boundary.

Suggest ways in which the author of each 'first' could improve further work.
Synthesize your learning of the process you have gone through in this task.
Be prepared to present your findings to the wider group.

The students gained a great deal from the activity, both individually and as CFGs, although they missed several key points that Steve brought out in the plenary:

- the standard of academic writing and its impact on grading, for example, mixed tenses, imprecise grammar and inaccurate use of punctuation;
- over-reliance on electronic sources for theoretical underpinning;
- inconsistency in referencing according to the Harvard format.

While these were, in Steve's experience, troublesome areas in the first year of the programme, he had found such use of exemplar material beneficial to undergraduates in having a positive influence on their subsequent written work.

He concluded the session by having each CFG:

- outline the key learning outcomes from the session;
- summarize the processes they had gone through in the session;
- explain how they would move their collective work forward as a result;
- explain how each student would move their individual project work forward as a result;
- summarize how their learning from the exemplar papers had developed their thoughts in the first session relating to what they needed to do in order to achieve the module outcomes.

The final weeks of blended learning tended to be difficult as two CFGs ceased meeting and there was less activity from the work on the VLE and a notable increase in the amount of individual email traffic. The final week produced six, rather than the anticipated eight letters to the tutor and next year's learners, although they gave Steve some tangible areas for development. Following the submission of final assignments, Steve summarized his own learning key points and areas for development from the module and the use of CFGs, with an emphasis on maintaining the impetus of CFGs and promoting the VLE, in a short (1000-word) paper which he sent to the students and shared with his BA colleagues at the next tutor development event.

In conclusion, action research is a tangible development of a teaching practitioner's core functions where refinements and improvements in teaching and learning, through curriculum design, development and evaluation of the learner experience at all stages, are planned, reflected on, shared with learners and colleagues, are counted as professional development and constitute a cyclical process of continual development over time. The following practical activity is designed to help you invigorate a focus for your own action research as you embrace these key concepts as part of your own development.

Practical activity

Two letters (after Cowan 1998)

Identify a group of learners you regularly work with and divide them into two sub-groups – tutor and student.

Each member of the tutor sub-group is to write a paragraph suggesting how you can improve your teaching and/or their learning. The sub-group then collaborates on the production of a letter that encompasses their collective thoughts and suggestions.

Each member of the student sub-group is to write a paragraph to a new student starting the same course next year. The paragraph is to be as helpful as possible by offering advice on how the new student can gain most benefit from the course, identifying in advance a key hurdle they may face and outlining the positive outcomes from studying the course. Likewise, the sub-group then collaborates on the production of a letter that encompasses their collective thoughts and suggestions.

Using the two letters produced by the group as a basis for your own action research (after Elliott 1991):

- identify an area or aspects of the course or programme that can be improved;
- draw up a general plan of how you can improve those key aspects;
- list three steps or actions required to achieve the improvements;
- identify ways in which you can monitor their implementation and effects;
- identify a critical friend who you can share your plan with before, during and after this first cycle of research;
- decide how you could disseminate the findings (improvements and areas for further refinement) with your colleagues.

7

Reflective practice and continuing professional development

Robinson (2009: 1) defines CPD as, 'a framework of learning and development which contributes to continued effectiveness as a professional', a definition which is atypical of others who benefit from a clear understanding of CPD, human resources (previously known as 'personnel' when we were seen as people) and LLS management. Yet the notion of a *framework* immediately threatens to systematize CPD and brews a heady mix of potential conflict and tension comprising regulation, uncertainty, performativity, instability and institutionalism. The undercurrent to such dark thoughts and suspicions is then easily located alongside the notion that, for many reasons, there is no longer a 'job for life' especially in a teaching or training role in our fragmented and casualized sector. As briefly discussed in Chapter 1, successive Governmental tinkering in the sector has raised CPD and reflective practice from a privileged position to one where we can be forgiven for thinking of them in such terms, and especially of surveillance – do your CPD and reflect on it and you get a box ticked. Therefore, if you take nothing else from this book at least take this: the person best placed to identify your CPD needs is you. You should negotiate your ideas, options and plans with your supervisor, but the development is about you and your professional practice. Again, who is the person best placed *to think, meditate or ponder* (Hanks 1979) on the effectiveness of your teaching practice? We rest our case.

Similarly, be reminded that a teaching and learning organization's greatest asset is its staff so, while reflecting on developing your practice, think also about achieving your potential and being open to opportunities that look inviting.

While reflecting on yourself, also learn about yourself – think about how you think, how you learn and of the things that interest you; think about your development and potential in such a way that it becomes natural, easy, long term and incremental as you grow in your role as a teaching professional; and think about the impact you are making on your learners. Thus, thought of in these ways, CPD is far from being a tool of surveillance.

Appraisal

A useful starting point is the appraisal process where your organization will very likely have a staff appraisal policy (or similar review process) that seeks to systematize teachers' achievements and development, using a range of data, as part of a continuous review process. While this can occasionally bear passing resemblance to a team's SAR (see Chapter 4), it is decidedly personal and confidential and will be carried out in the sanctuary of a professional discussion with your curriculum manager or similar supervisor. We can perhaps clarify this by taking an overview of what is, and is not, appraisal.

Appraisal is:

- driven by reflective thought;
- a formal review of your personal achievements over the last year;
- an opportunity to discuss personal, professional and career development aspirations and opportunities;
- a two-way discussion (which you should lead);
- positive and constructive;
- an opportunity for improved communication and shared understanding.

Appraisal is not:

- about surprises or being talked at;
- an opportunity for your supervisor to increase your workload in any way;
- an opportunity for your supervisor to moan about your colleagues, etc.;
- about always reaching agreement;
- a once-a-year paper exercise;
- focused on statistical data;
- something that you need to be defensive about;
- the only time in the year when you can sit down and really discuss with your supervisor things that concern or encourage you.

When approached in this way, appraisal is concerned with establishing your potential, improving job satisfaction and negotiating your professional development. You should be given plenty of advance notice of the appraisal process and time to think about the issues and developments you wish to bring to the discussion. Here, it is especially beneficial preparation to invest time in reflecting on the year, not just recent events, and to have deliberate ideas about the things you want to discuss regarding your development. This is a classic example of reflecting both backwards and forwards where the focus is on your training and development needs and the support that you need to achieve them in the light of the last year or so.

The following is meant to be neither an exhaustive or prescriptive list of discussion topics at appraisal, but a list of prompts to help you think about you for a change as you prepare for your appraisal:

- How accurate is your job description? (Does it need changing?)
- What have you done well this year? (Do you know why and how?)
- What have you enjoyed this year?
- What difference/impact have you made? (Learners? Team? Other communities of practice? Is there evidence of this?)
- What has been difficult for you to achieve this year? (Why so?)
- What can you now do that you could not do this time last year?
- What have you not enjoyed this year? (What had you anticipated?)
- What has helped (or hindered) you in your work this year?
- You came into the teaching profession for a reason – are you still here for the same reason? (What, if anything, has changed?)
- How could you make a greater impact on learning/the learner experience than last year? (How could you know/recognize a greater impact?)
- What could you do better next year? (What skills or support do you need? Who or what could help?)
- What training could help you do your job better?
- Do you have any assumptions that you have not challenged or critically explored?
- Are there other areas of your job/team/organization that you would like to develop into further? (What skills or knowledge would you need? Who could help?)

In summary, think about the gap between 'what is' and 'what could be' and take ownership of how to close the gap through reflection that leads towards meaningful CPD.

As mentioned in Chapter 1, we are in the privileged position of wearing the two hats that the sector values – simultaneously being a professional in our vocational, occupational or subject specialist area and a professional of teaching and learning, a duality that is often referred to as *dual professionalism* (Orr and Simmons 2009). In much the same way as other professional bodies or institutes represent our vocational interests at the macro level, the IfL acts as our professional body as teaching specialists to lobby Parliament on our behalf, produce journals regularly to keep us updated with current issues regarding our specialism and make informed suggestions about our CPD. Given the particular nuances of our dual professional status, the IfL suggest a model for CPD which draws on three areas or domains:

1   *Subject specialism* Many of us were recruited for the currency of our up-to-date subject-specialist knowledge, a unique and often rare component of our individual identity that is much in demand in the sector. One of the major tensions of coming off the shop floor (or wherever we came from) into teaching is maintaining the same level of knowledge and which Cowan (1998: 29) posits well

thus: 'It has been stated that the half life of an electronic engineer is about two years. In other words, within two years the effectiveness of an electronic engineer has deteriorated by half.' While other specialist areas will differ in terms of how far we slip behind in two years, the danger of losing the currency of our specialist knowledge is a compelling reason for the IfL to include this domain as one of the three components of our CPD.

2   *Teaching and learning*   In the same way that we need to maintain the currency of our subject specialist knowledge, so we also need to maintain our specialist status as teachers. For example, all of us are outstanding with at least one teaching and learning strategy yet we also know that we need to provide variety, stretch, challenge and support in our teaching that does not come from reliance on a single teaching and learning approach. Likewise, new technologies are opening new avenues to what is possible for teaching our specialisms, assessing its learning in innovative and engaging ways and invigorating the learning of those who are increasingly becoming digital natives (Prensky 2001) for whom electronic resources and approaches are the norm.

Another way to think of this might be to ask yourself the sort of questions that could come out of having just been observed by an Ofsted inspector; for example, how do I move from 'good' to 'outstanding'? What are the skills that I need to develop? What have I not yet tried? What am I afraid of trying? What might 'risk-taking' look like with this group? To what extent do I draw on their workplace experiences?

3   *Context and policy*   This is arguably the most difficult of the three domains in that many of us think that policy and context are not our remit, where policy is devised by educational policymakers who appear to know nothing of teaching and learning, and even less about the social and emotional baggage that our learners bring to class each morning, and that context is directed and managed by the SMT or similar and we merely 'deliver' what they can get funding for. Whatever the truth of such a perspective, there are other lenses through which we can view policy and context. For example, an engineering tutor collaborating with other departments where the BTEC media students video the tutor turning a flanged bush, send the video to the OCR Level 2 team whose students convert the recording to DVD, which is used by the engineering tutor in a classroom and posted on the college VLE. Similarly, ICT-related students can be used to video live tutor demonstrations that are difficult for all learners to see, for example a carpentry and joinery class learning how to fit a door lock, in situ, with a media student recording the process and projecting it onto a large screen.

Aside from cross-organization collaboration there are opportunities for team-focused development (e.g. preparing for inspection two years, rather than two weeks, before); sharing resources and web videos with colleagues; taking responsibility for developing a serious strategy for encouraging Black and minority ethnic (BME) groups into your programme area; presenting findings from action research projects (see Chapter 6), BA dissertation or modular work and findings of your recent networking with local or partner colleges – 'This is what the competition are up to', etc.

Similarly, Awarding Bodies, despite the alleged levelness of the playing field, are often doing very different things and it is worthwhile researching what these are doing or planning to do.

One of the most beneficial, but ignored, sources of activity in this domain is to go out and see what employers want us to be doing. Most employers are too busy trying to stay in business and their training needs are often low on the agenda, especially when bumping along the bottom of a recession, and many probably have little idea of what you can offer. To find out, reflect on it and share it with your team is very good CPD.

Thus, we offer three case studies as a useful way of exploring what is possible in the diverse sector in which we work.

Case study 1: the police officer

John has served as a police officer for 28 years, the last eight in the role of firearms instructor, and he completed a Certificate in Education three years ago. While the teaching qualification was ostensibly to refine his instructional role, his main motivation was to gain certification that would permit him access to an FE teaching role, probably in public services, when he retires from the police service next year. During his 'dog and tennis ball' reflection at the end of each shift, John has recently been thinking about his current role, the things that he still wants to achieve and the looming prospect of realizing his ambition to transfer to FE. Although John takes new challenges in his stride, he is also mindful that he knows little of what to expect with teenage learners and has been casting his thoughts around trying to assemble some options.

During his recent annual review with his superior where the prospect of retirement and cost savings were discussed, John shared his thoughts, prospects and CPD options and gained permission to work on a voluntary basis with the local FE college with a view to improving public relations.

As a member of a private shooting club, he has met someone who teaches sport and recreation at the college and has been introduced to the curriculum manager for public services at the college who has welcomed his suggested contribution. John views his midweek off-duty time as opportunities to get a foot in the door at the college through a volunteering role, initially to give a guest lecture to the BTEC public service groups on the role and training of the firearms officer. During informal discussions with, and at the suggestion of, the college curriculum manager he has joined the IfL, registered his intention to achieve QTLS status and has thought carefully about how to make a gradual transition between the two contextual areas while maintaining his current post. While his current employer does not require him to formally register his CPD plans, John has initially identified the following 30+ hours of CPD activities for the next year, a development plan which carries the blessing of his seniors in both contexts:

Subject specialism
research/study the BTEC public services curriculum including core texts;
collaborate with college peers in work shadowing, curriculum design and evaluation
   and reflect on the experiences;
research the accuracy of the American boat-tailed round for police use.

Teaching and learning
on a voluntary basis, team teach and support learners on the public services course;
research appropriate teaching, learning and assessment strategies for 16–18 learners;
carry out informal observations of peers teaching in both police and college settings;
reflect on the differences between BTEC and police learners with regards to motivation, physical fitness, approaches to effective learning and cultural dispositions.

Policy and context
research quality standards and systems in the LLS;
attend the end of year staff development event at the college;
reflect on the differences between teaching roles in the police and LLS;
complete own QTLS portfolio.

Case study 2: the ex-nurse

Sam is well versed in the ethos and culture of CPD and mentoring since the mind-
1990s having been trained as an ICU (Intensive Care Unit) nurse, converting her
nursing diploma to a nursing honours degree through further higher study and later
retraining as a Tier 2 mental health practitioner. Two years ago, in the wake of Strategic
Health Authority restructuring and the contracting-out of mental health care, Sam
took voluntary redundancy and now works for one of the contracted agencies as one
of two mental health awareness coordinators. Her role seems to have been constantly
developing in response to the needs of clients and the stakeholders, and currently
combines training and assessing community-based Tier 1 care staff in the workplace,
the promotion of mental health awareness with various stakeholders and providing
employability skills training for clients at a day care centre in the community. Over the
last two years, Sam has been enculturated into both the agency and the workings of
the key stakeholders and prefers the twin training roles which continue to grow with
the prospect of developing into a full-time position when her job share colleague
retires next year. Sam finds it fruitful to reflect back during the 30-minute drive home
each day and the morning journey helps her to focus on the coming day, and she has
a close circle of trusted and critical healthcare peers who she meets with fortnightly
as a social group to 'talk shop'. Reflecting on her experiences since her last year's
appraisal, she believes that her individual teaching performance is well advanced but
becoming stifled through other competing demands in her constantly developing
role. One particular and unanticipated demand on her time has been supporting the
language and literacy needs of some of the care staff, many of whom were recruited
from overseas and who especially struggle with NVQ jargon.

   At her recent annual appraisal, Sam took the opportunity to discuss with her
manager the dynamic nature of the coordinator role, her career trajectory and her
developmental preferences and was encouraged to plan for a full-time training and
assessment role. Here, the manager realized the benefits of Sam consolidating and
standardizing the skills set that she has established throughout the agency while leaving
the promotional duties to another member of staff who wished to develop into that
area. Sam spent a month reflecting on the skills that she needed to develop, discussed
them informally with a number of trusted peers and returned to her supervisor with a

staged 'first thoughts' two year CPD plan, her rationale being that she wanted to see the overall picture but also the separate steps she would need to take. Sam also thought that it would be useful to formally revisit the progress of her development at least every six months, rather than annually, through collaboration and dialogue with her supervisor based on her ongoing reflections. Notably, Sam had a clear idea that she wanted to develop her colleagues and learners, particularly those who could effectively mentor, support and assess new staff, and proposed the following CPD plan for herself:

Subject specialism

6 months: research theories of mentoring carers in mental health settings;
research current strategies for managing mental health issues arising from care work for Tier 1 practitioners.

12 months: research emerging theories relating to mental health care for children and young people;
network with children and young people's agencies to identify best practice and current trends.

18 months: research emerging theories relating to how mental health clients learn in community settings;
update knowledge relating to cognitive behaviour therapy.

2 years: research recent developments in dementia care to extend clients' independence and reflect on implications/benefits for the agency;
research the efficacy of current theories relating to NLP (neuro-linguistic programming) in mental health settings.

Teaching and learning

6 months: enrol on a Professional Graduate Certificate in Education course;
Complete the V1 verifier award;
research available resources for supporting language and literacy skills.

12 months: learn how to utilise WebCT more effectively in order to have all T&L resources available electronically on the agency intranet;
produce an in-house basic mentor training programme.

18 months: produce an in-house enhanced mentor training programme.

2 years: set up critical friendship groups/learning sets amongst agency staff;
Produce pilot CPD programme for learning sets.

Policy and context

6 months: join the IfL;
research early findings and trends in the contracting-out of mental health care in other regions and consider the implications for own agency.

12 months: mentor two care staff through A1 assessor awards;
consolidate, and disseminate to peers, key issues from research over the last 6 months.

18 months: set up and host a quarterly employer/stakeholder forum for professional dialogue on key trends, policy initiatives, sharing best practice and reflective practice.

2 years: mentor two care staff through V1 verifier awards;
register for QTLS.

Case study 3: the musician

Ranvir is a semi-professional musician who has recently turned to teaching, for some financial stability, in the employment of a specialist music college where she teaches part time with 12 hours class contact each week. Her twin specialist areas of singing and classical piano equip her to teach both theoretical and practical aspects of popular music, musical theatre, performance techniques and subject specialist investigation on the National Diploma in Popular Music. One of the requirements of accepting the vacant post was to achieve a Post-Graduate Certificate in Education (PGCE) at Masters level and she is currently nearing the end of the programme. Ranvir has no experience of formalized CPD but is a firm believer in informal development through several communities of practice to which she belongs. In particular, she found the reflective component of her PGCE refreshingly useful since it ranged much wider than just her teaching skill development and she now finds it natural and easy (while relaxing to South American folk music) to reflect on other dimensions of her specialism and context. She has also recently discovered the benefits of recording her introspective thoughts of critical incidents in a small journal which she regularly revisits because it sits well with her reflective stance, gives her ready access to previous quite deep thoughts and gives a sense of distance travelled in her journey.

Here, on reflecting on her transition into teaching, she has found assistance with particular pieces of music and techniques through informal trading of instrumental information in the staff room (indeed, most of the staffroom dialogue has been about teaching and learning and she has found this useful and encouraging); she has begun to better appreciate that creativity needs to be balanced with theory and technical study as she has worked with her own band to produce new music; and she has also become more critically appreciative of other music genres and techniques while sharing music venues with other bands. Yet she also feels that her instructional style in one-to-one music practice sessions is not having the impact on learners that she expects since they all, it seems, require far more repetition from her than she ever needed when in their place, yet they have been reluctant to discuss this with her. Another concern for her is that she has yet to 'get up to speed' with the way ICT is used throughout the college and feels that her colleagues exploit its use more. Here, Ranvir had convinced herself that this was due to her part-time position but now accepts, if only to herself, that this is more an excuse than a reason.

In negotiation with her curriculum manager, she has joined the IfL, registered her intention to achieve QTLS status and has identified 15 hours of CPD activities for the next year as follows:

Subject specialism
learn grade 3 standard pieces and reflect on the experience;
attend two musicals, two operas and two arena performances this year – critically analyse how expression and emotion are effectively conveyed and how they can be embedded more in the BTEC programme;
release own third album and reflect on how the experience can be used as a learning resource in college.

Teaching and learning

attend training for Interactive Whiteboards and Wallwisher;

video self teaching a session in music practice in order to reflect on, and evaluate, own tutorial technique through the lens of the learner/observer;

make time/try different strategies during individual music practice sessions to encourage learners to give feedback on my own development as a teacher.

Policy and context

become proficient in the use of electronic registers;

become proficient in the use of the new electronic recording system (ProMonitor) for assessments;

compile own QTLS portfolio and reflect on own distance travelled over three years.

Thanks to central Government (Ofsted 2003; 2009) CPD, and therefore reflective practice, have become regulated by and systematized through the IfL and John, Sam and Ranvir need to record their previous year's CPD. The following rough guide is designed for those who, like them, have never done so before.

Recording your CPD on the IfL REfLECT online system

REfLECT is a useful tool, having many features that you can utilize to make the most of your development; for example, an online storage space for resources and session plans and CV builder, etc. We are concerned here with a simple step-by-step guide to recording and declaring your CPD hours in order to conform to the IfL's minimum requirements, although the system does much more and you should explore it when you have time. One way to begin to understand REfLECT is to think of recording your CPD as a system of files and folders, much like arranging Word files, where the following apply:

- An **activity** is a CPD event which you discuss reflectively in a sort of file. You use a separate file for each activity which, when completed, becomes known as an **asset**.

- A **CPD record** is like a folder to which you send your completed assets.

- A **tag** is part of a labelling system to categorize each activity or asset, e.g. *Subject Specialism; Learning and Teaching*; and *Institutional Context* (these are very close to the three IfL domains although why they are not identical is unclear).

- A **pad** is a small window that contains either instructions or a text box which you write in. The text boxes take some getting used to and, with time, you might find it useful to draft your CPD assets as Word files from which you cut and paste onto the REfLECT pads.

Recording your CPD activites in the form of assets stored in a CPD record should be ongoing rather than a last-minute dash to meet your CPD deadline and is simply a process of you storing entries that you will use later to declare your CPD. Here, declaring your CPD is like uploading the folder so that the CPD hours for the assets or files are credited against your membership requirement. A good tip: do not use speech marks when writing in REfLECT (see later).

To use REfLECT:

(LC denotes 'left click' on the mouse)

Log in on the IfL website at: www.ifl.ac.uk

Down the Left-hand side of the front page are a number of links. LC on REfLECT
to reveal your current **assets**.

(If you have never recorded any CPD activity the **pad** on the right will have '0'
against the number of **assets** [files] in your electronic storage space or **asset store**,
therefore you will not have a CPD record [folder], and you need to create one from
the outset as follows.)

To create a CPD record:

At the bottom of the screen are four buttons.

LC on **create new** to reveal a curved menu of options.

LC on **more** will reveal others including **CPD record**.

LC on **CPD record** and you will notice that you are on the first of five pages. (You
can work through them in any order and when you close the record it should automatically save. You can revisit and edit any asset or CPD record later.)

Page 1 requires you to give a **title** to the CPD record, e.g. 'CPD Record 2012–13'.
The **tag** options may not be relevant, since the CPD record should contain assets
which embrace all three domains, so ignore it for the moment if you wish.

The **description** text box requires a brief description of what the CPD record
contains, e.g. 'Collection of CPD-related assets from September 2012–August 2013'.
(Either LC on the second button or LC the right arrow at the bottom to take you to
the next page).

Page 2 asks you to **choose a template**. The template is a well presented version of the
assets that you enter later and is a pleasant surprise at the end of the process. LC on
one of the formats from the menu.

Page 3 asks you to state the **required amount of hours for this CPD record** by
typing it into the small window (this is the minimum number of annual hours stipu-
lated by the IfL according to your work role), e.g. 24.

LC on the two **start** and **finish** calendars below to make clear the period of the CPD
activities. (LC on the left arrow of the start calendar to find the month and year, then
LC on the date which automatically appears in the window. The finish date is set at
today's date but can be changed in the same way.)

Page 4 asks for your **reflections** on the range of activities or assets you intend to store
in the CPD record or folder and it may be appropriate to enter 'not yet' in the
box and return to it later in order to edit it after you have thought about them
collectively.

A typical reflection at this point might be something like:

This period of CPD activities represents some significant shifts for me.

*First, my developments in my subject specialism have focused on updating my employability-
related skills through various research and networking events in the light of recent trends in
the Information and Guidance Sector, particularly the recent theories surrounded CV
building and interview techniques and the restructuring of the Connexions service.*

Second, my CPD activities regarding teaching and learning have included peer observations, independent reading and collaboration with other specialists across the college. While much of the focus has been driven by the need to better manage challenging behaviour, there have been significant benefits to the overall learner experience of my groups with a positive impact on learner engagement, stretch and challenge, differentiation, retention and achievement.

Third, I have developed an increased understanding and appreciation of the many tensions at work in the sector through independent reading, institution-wide CPD events, collaboration with the construction trades tutors and through monitoring developments invigorated by the new coalition government.

Below this text box there is a prompt asking if you wish to **Record time spent on this activity?** Again, you may decide to return to this later after you have added up the total number of hours for the various CPD activities you intend to store as **assets** in this folder or **CPD record**.

The final page asks what you would like to do with this CPD record. For the moment, LC on the green tick to save and close the folder/record.

You will be back at the **current REfLECT activity** page and the activity **pad** on the right will have '1' against the number of **assets** (files) in your electronic storage space or **asset store**, the CPD record now being counted as an asset. Do not be confused by this – just accept it.

LC on **1 asset in your asset store** and a new pad will appear on the left with the title you gave to your CPD record/folder, e.g. 'CPD Record 2012–13'.

LC on the title and a new pad will appear on the right asking **what would you like to do?** LC on **view this asset** and it will appear on the left in the promised, much-improved format you chose earlier (and if you used speech marks as you entered text this will now be garbled). Remember that this is the folder that is to contain the various individual CPD activities as assets. Close this pad (LC on the X icon at the top), close the **view assets** pad (LC on the X icon at the top) and you will be back at the **current REfLECT activity** page and ready to create an asset.

To create an **asset**:

LC on the **create new** button and select **activity** from the curved menu for a new pad to appear. (At the bottom of the pad are four buttons, representing a separate page for the same activity, and an arrow pointing to the right in the same way as when creating the CPD record. The No. 1 button will be highlighted meaning that you are on the first of four pages which, again, you can move through in any order, save and revisit as with the CPD record.)

Starting at the first page, a **title** box appears in a new pad asking for a title of the activity you wish to record, e.g. 'Peer observation'

Below the title box is a **tag** box. Click on the arrow next to it and it will reveal three options so that you can categorize the activity, e.g. **Learning and Teaching**. (LC on Learning and Teaching saves you typing it in.)

The larger box below offers you the opportunity to give a brief **description** of the activity (not a detailed reflective account of it – this comes later). Type in something that makes clear the individual nature of that particular peer observation so that you can easily find it when you wish to, e.g. 'Observation of Bev's session – 17/3/13 – Employability Skills (Entry level 2)'.

LC on the arrow will open a new pad (page 2) which asks you three questions.

First, **reason(s) for undertaking this activity** should be straightforward to comment on in the space, e.g. *To observe how Bev manages challenging behaviour.*

Second, LC on **knowledge/skills gained** brings up the next part of the page to type to, e.g. *Appropriately challenging latecomers; setting a positive feel during the introduction; how to be firm but fair; subtle ways of using language to maintain learner engagement; use of praise and reward; frequent changes of pairings and activities.*

Third, LC on **what was the impact of the activity?** brings up the final part of the page where you type in your brief thoughts about the impact that the activity has had on the learning that goes on in your own sessions. E.g. *Improved learner behaviours in terms of punctuality, engagement, social skills and motivation.*

You conclude the pad by picking the date from the calendar menu at the bottom or clicking the **ongoing** button (where the activity or asset is part of something long-term, for example a BA course).

LC on the right arrow again will bring in page 3, which is for you to record your detailed reflections, having reflected on the activity and the impact. For example: *This has been an enormous boost for me. The first thing I noticed was how much less stressful my Entry level sessions became when I changed activities more and mixed up the pairings and groups – they seemed to have a new urgency, were more competitive, worked harder than me, responded well to praise and I didn't need to shout once. (I made a point of following Bev's style by making sure that each learner was praised for something, although a couple of them clearly found this strange, but didn't over-do it.) The other thing I've noticed is that, because I don't single out latecomers in front of the class now but catch them at the next break in activities, punctuality has improved – like they've had their audience taken away so they turn up on time and look for another opportunity to steal the limelight which they don't get because the others are too busy. Here's where the use of positive language seems to come in, although I have a lot to learn and refine in this department, where I sort of impose a 'can do' attitude rather than the usual 'I can't do this – it's too hard'. I've been saying things like, 'when you've done this we can get onto . . .' rather than, 'if you do this then we can get onto . . .'. The results are amazing because there's hardly any moaning, resistance and distraction now.*

LC on **record time spent on this activity?** at the bottom of the pad, enter the number of hours in the small window and LC on **arose from my CPD plan**. LC on the green tick to save and close the pad at this point.

LC on the right arrow again will bring up the fourth and final page which asks you **what would you like to do next?** with this asset (there are five options). Moving the cursor over **send to** highlights another menu with six options. LC on **CPD record** and the CPD record you created earlier will be listed in the pad on the right.

LC on CPD Record 2012–13 then LC on the green tick.

The CPD record (folder) will appear, along with the description you gave earlier, and the asset you just created listed below as the first CPD event in the record or folder. Beneath these you will see a **Reviewing** pane which states the minimum number of CPD hours you need to record, the number of hours recorded to date and the number of hours tagged (i.e. number of hours in each of the three IfL domains).

Returning to the **current REfLECT activity** page will reveal that you have **two assets in your asset store**. Continue to record individual CPD activities as new assets throughout the year until the time comes for you to declare your CPD.

To declare your CPD:

(This section, or third stage, is concerned solely with ensuring that the CPD record you have generated and populated with assets is correct, reflects what you want it to and is sent to the IfL in accordance with the requirements for retaining your professional standing in the sector.)

Start at the **current REfLECT activity** page. LC on the **tools** button at the bottom and a curved menu will appear. LC on **CPD declaration** and a new pad appears on the right with three pages.

The first page tells you the status of your CPD records, i.e. whether you have shared this with anyone (which you can do) and the date that you last declared your CPD to the IfL, which will probably be between June and August last year (but will be blank if this is the first time). You do not need to do anything to this page if the details are correct.

The second page lists information regarding your **work context** and can be updated, if required, by LC on the pencil icon on the right. If the data is correct you do not need to do anything to this page either.

The third page is concerned with the hours you need to declare (or have already declared) this year in the June – August window when this must be done. Check that the hours are correct. Under **add my hours from this CPD record** you LC on the arrow to the right of the window and LC on the appropriate CPD record for this year (if this is the first time then there will be only one listed).

Hours recorded in Reflect should show a figure equal to the combined hours for all the assets you sent to your CPD record. If there are other CPD events or activities that you have benefited from this year, but not created assets for, LC on the next window and type in those combined hours.

The **Total hours declared in this period** will have increased and should be a correct summative amount of hours.

LC on **View and review CPD declaration** and a new window opens asking whether you wish to send the CPD declaration to the IfL (**Send to IfL**), to close the declaration without saving it (**Close**) or to cancel and return to Page 3 (**Cancel**). LC on **Send to IfL** and a new window opens to display an overview of your hours, both required and declared, on REfLECT headed paper. At the top right is a grey rectangular button entitled **Send my declaration** which you LC on.

Close the CPD declaration pad (LC on the X icon at the top) and you are back at the **current REfLECT activity** pad. LC on **View**, then **My assets**, will reveal that you have an extra asset in your asset store, this being a receipt of the declaration on the headed paper confirming that your CPD record has been sent to the IfL.

Practical activity

Reflecting back:

Thinking about your job role over the last 12 months, consider what you would include as assets if you were about to register your development using REfLECT. We suggest that one way to do this might be to:

1   recreate the Venn diagram (see Figure 7.1) on a flip chart;

2   populate the diagram with your 'first thoughts';

3   reflect on what you have written, e.g. what is missing; what was the most beneficial to your development; what has made the greatest impact on your learners; in which domain have you been most/least active; is there a reason for this; what are the trends; are you heading in the direction you want to go? etc. See also the prompts under 'Appraisal Process' earlier in this chapter;

4   use different highlight pens to identify the greatest impact, the most beneficial and the areas for further development, etc;

5   put the hours for each alongside each point and see how they sit with the IfL requirements according to your work role

     (you are not aiming for a perfect 33.3 per cent split between the three domains but you will have points in all three domains);

6   share your thoughts with a critical friend or your supervisor.

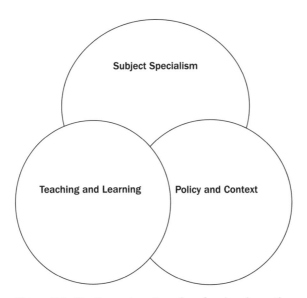

Figure 7.1 The three domains of professional practice

Reflecting forward:

Thinking about your job role and the organization in which you will work over the next 12 months, consider the following and write key points on separate sticky notes:

- What imposed changes are likely?
- How might such changes be accommodated?
- What other changes would you like to see?
- How would you like your role to develop?
- What are the recent developments in your subject specialist area?
- What new skills and knowledge would you need?
- How could you develop those skills and knowledge?
- Who and what could help you?
- What would you like to be doing in two years' time?
- What would you like to be doing in five years' time?

Arrange the sticky notes into the three categories:

1   subject specialism
2   teaching and learning
3   institution, policy and context.

Reflect on what the notes are telling you, for example, is that an accurate picture? Is it the way I want things to be? What is missing? What will the impact be on me/my learners/my organization? Etc.

Recommended reading

www.ifl.ac.uk (The website is open to non-members and offers guidance and tips on key development issues in your role.)

www.cpdinstitute.org.uk (Another source of guidance and resources relating to wider CPD issues.)

8

Problems and limitations in engaging in reflective practice

Though the principle of the engagement in reflective practice is a well established one in teaching, the process of reflecting on practice is not without its problems and limitations. In this chapter they will be grouped and discussed under two main headings: 'engagement in reflective practice' and 'culture and reflective practice'

Engagement in reflective practice

The first issue with engagement is the problem of actually starting to reflect on practice. Several writers, notably Husu et al. (2008) and Korthagen (2001) argue that many student teachers are reluctant to engage in reflection because they do not know how to. This may seem a rather obvious point, but Korthagen argues that there is an assumption that student teachers 'just know' how to reflect and what to reflect on, and that is not necessarily the case. Suter (2007) found that some student teachers lacked the confidence to start reflecting on practice, stating that their vocational training and experience to date had not required them to reflect on practice, and in some instances discouraged reflection. He quotes a student teacher, Gary, who spent over twenty years in the Royal Navy:

> I am a can-do kind of guy, you have to be in the Services, something comes up, you deal with it . . . you have got to consider that I spent over twenty years in the Royal Navy . . . I only finished my service four years ago. Writing down thoughts is still a bit too touchy feely for me . . .

Gary felt that he had not been encouraged to reflect on practice during his time in the armed services, and that as a result he was finding the process difficult to engage with as a student teacher. Suter notes that several student teachers were reluctant start the process of reflecting on practice because there was a suspicion that it was 'navel-gazing' and the important thing (in industry and in teaching) was to *do* something. He admits that as a teacher educator he had made an assumption that because he thought it was a 'good thing' the student teachers would think so too. Both Husu et al. (2008) and Korthagen (2001) argue that it is wrong to assume that student teachers will somehow 'naturally' both see the point of reflecting on practice and know how to reflect. They argue that it is important for the process of reflection to be 'modelled' by teacher educators and that structured guidance is offered to student teachers, especially in the early stages of their professional development.

The second issue where engagement in reflective practice is concerned is about *what* the teacher reflects on. Some writers (see for instance Usher and Edwards 1994) argue that it is not necessarily a problem to get teachers to reflect on their practice, but that the quality of that reflection can be. This problem is twofold. First some student teachers find it difficult to be sufficiently analytical in their reflections, especially where written reflections are concerned (Goldhill 2009). Their observations tend to be descriptive, so their reflections are a log of what happened in their professional practice with little consideration of why issues arise.

The other issue of quality of reflection might be termed 'impoverished reflective practice'. This is where the reflections are not informed by anything outside the immediate professional situation of the teacher doing the reflecting. Take for instance a student teacher teaching law in a further education college. He writes his reflections on his own teaching, in which are identified several issues that need to be addressed, including that of the passivity of the learners in his group. The teacher observes other teachers in his department, but finds the same low levels of learner activity as in his own group. He concludes that this is the 'norm' in the teaching and learning the department is engaged in. If the student teacher had cast his net wider, he might have found some ideas on increasing learner activity in other parts of the college. He might have supplemented this by reading the literature on good practice in encouraging active learning in the increasing number of books on teaching and learning in LLS, and the journals dedicated to the sector. Usher and Edwards (1994) argue that without recourse to this 'published knowledge' any reflection is 'uninformed', therefore any action taken as a result of this impoverished reflection is likely not to be effective as it might be.

There is another aspect of engagement in reflective practice which might be argued would result in an impoverished reflection on practice, that is 'strategic compliance'. In the context of education this was a term first used by Woods (1986) to describe those activities undertaken by the teacher without real commitment. He noted that teachers would complete tasks required of them by their superiors despite the perception that undertaking those tasks was not necessarily important for effective teaching and learning. Thus the teachers would 'comply' because not doing so would create conflict with managers. Shain and Gleeson (1999) and later Suter (2007) noted strategic compliance in their research in FE Education colleges. The writers noted that the changes brought about by the incorporation of FE colleges in the 1990s led to changes in the role and workloads of FE teachers. One response was to become 'strategic compliers', following directions from managers to undertake tasks which were not considered essential to the processes of teaching and learning. Shain and Gleeson noted that there were those who resisted what they considered to be the imposition of these tasks, but that did lead to conflict with managers. Suter noted a resentment in some of the teachers' responses to his questions on their roles and responsibilities, with one teacher stating: 'We joke in our staffroom that the teaching sometimes gets in the way of the paperwork, but I seriously wonder sometimes whether I am employed as a teacher or an admin. assistant.' Suter found that the role of the teacher was changing to include responsibilities not deemed essential to teaching and learning. This resulted in strategic compliance and perfunctory treatment of what was seen as the 'paperwork'. Of greater concern here is that Suter noted an attitude of strategic compliance towards the process of reflective practice in his teacher education students. These were teachers already employed, mostly full time, in the LLS. Suter found that some (but by no means all) of the teacher education students, while not refusing or even questioning the need to engage in reflective practice, would do so 'minimally', writing enough to satisfy the bare requirements for reflection.

Why might strategic compliance extend to the process of reflective practice? It is after all concerned with the process of teaching and learning. There are several factors which are important in understanding this. First there is the issue of time. The changes in the role and responsibilities of the teacher mentioned above have tended to increase the workload of the teacher. Avis et al. (2001) examined the work logs that they asked teachers to keep on their work activities. They were struck by both the variety of tasks undertaken by the teacher in any single day as well as the amount of work. There was not just the teaching itself, but the preparation for teaching, the tracking of learners, records of learners to be kept, meetings called by managers as well as development activities. It is understandable that in professional situations where there is a very high work tempo some teachers feel that they do not have enough time for systematic reflection on practice.

In circumstances where the teacher in the LLS has a myriad of tasks to perform during the working day, it may very well be that the only time for systematic reflection on practice is in the teacher's own time. To do this takes personal commitment from the individual teacher. If the individual is not fully convinced of the efficacy of reflection on practice, there is a danger that the reflection which is undertaken will be minimal, perhaps only enough to satisfy the requirements of a teacher education course or of the teacher's professional body. There is some evidence that we should not take it for granted that teachers and student teachers will have that personal commitment to reflection on practice. Hobbs (2007) noted a reluctance for student teachers to fully engage in reflection on practice, particularly in situations where the reflections were to be assessed as part of a teacher education course. She found there was a danger – if the perception of the student teachers was that the reflection was 'forced' of provoking a 'strategic response' to reflection on practice. Hobbs found for instance that some student teachers would write the bare minimum in their reflective journal, or leave whole sections out. The strategic response exhibited itself in another way, one that should cause concern for any teacher educator. Hobbs noted that some student teachers were reluctant to look critically at their own teaching because they might be 'marked down' by the tutor. The danger here is that the student teacher is not looking honestly at their own practice in an effort to make their teaching more effective, which of course is one of the main purposes of reflection on practice. Goldhill (2009) noted that the trainees who were the subject of her research were 'inhibited' in their reflections because of 'deep seated fears of getting it wrong'.

It may be that the strategic response to reflection on practice in situations where the reflections are part of the assessment of student teachers can be and no doubt is being addressed by teacher educators, something we will return to at the end of this chapter.

The last aspect of the process of engagement with reflective practice concerns the actual professional situation the teacher finds her or himself in. Situational learning theorists have argued (see Lave and Wenger 1991) that what is learned and how it is learned is in large part dependent upon the nature of the workplace. We will discuss the 'cultural' issues relating to reflective practice in depth below, but it is worth noting here that the attitude towards the process of reflective practice in a particular professional situation is likely to influence the commitment of the individual teacher or student teacher to reflect on practice.

Reflective practice and the culture of the LLS

The last section finished by acknowledging the influence of the particular professional situation on the engagement in reflective practice of the teacher in LLS. In this section we will explore those cultural aspects of the sector which may have an influence on whether first there is likely to be any meaningful reflection on practice, and second whether reflective practice can actually benefit teachers and learners in FE. We will start with an outline of the cultural aspects of the LLS as a whole before going on to a discussion of the aspects of organizational culture which may limit the effectiveness of reflective practice.

Several commentators on the LLS have argued that changes brought about by government policy on FE in the 1980s and 1990s had a great effect on professional identity and culture. Ainley and Bailey (1997), Avis (1999, 2003), Hodkinson (1998) and Randle and Brady (1997) have all pointed to decisions taken by government between 1985 and 1992 as being particularly influential. Ainley and Bailey argue that a 'business model' was imposed on FE, with an emphasis on meeting 'customer needs', and describe the increasing influence of employers on the sector. Avis notes that particularly after the 'incorporation' of FE colleges in 1992 there has been an emphasis on the efficient use of resources, which includes teachers. Hodkinson argues that teachers have become more like technicians, stating:

> In English training organisations and colleges . . . a good teacher or trainer is someone who will work uncritically within whatever contexts are determined for her/him and in ways which are prescribed by others. Such teachers and trainers have the responsibility to succeed, but without the power and resources necessary to bring that success about.
>
> (Hodkinson 1998: 200)

It has been argued that this attitude towards teachers and their work has been influenced by a 'managerial discourse', a discourse being a system of ideas, which once established becomes difficult to challenge. These ideas include those drawn from the business world, that learners (and their sponsors) are the 'customers' of the education and training organizations. To best meet the needs of the customers efficient and effective use must be made of the resources of the organization, including the human resources. Efficient and effective use is made of resources only if they are managed properly. Effective management then includes the direction of staff, including teachers, by their managers. Avis et al. (2010: 210) argue that: 'the move towards managerialism undermines previous forms of control . . . it also accents the division between management and teachers as well as highlighting potential antagonisms surrounding professional autonomy'.

Randle and Brady (1997) noted the issue of what they saw as an erosion of professional autonomy. They argued that post–incorporation one model of management had been superseded by another. The 'public service' model emphasized teacher collegiality in decision making, a certain professional autonomy for the teacher and a trust that the teacher would use professional judgment in the conduct of their work and in the best interests of the learners. This, Randle and Brady argue, conflicts with the 'resource' model. The model emphasizes a 'customer' focus, managerial control over decision making, the deployment of resources including human resources and measurement of performance. Other writers since have noted the influence in what might be termed a 'business' model on the LLS (see Hodkinson and James 2003; Williams 2003; Gleeson et al. 2005)

How might this managerialism with its emphasis on control and measurement have an effect on the process of reflective practice in the LLS? Suter (2007) noted in student teachers the effects of the organizational culture influenced by the managerialist model. He found that some student teachers felt constrained by the relationship with their manager. One of them stated:

> I've had a few ideas about some changes we could make to the course [on which the student teacher taught]. They involve changing the length of some of the sessions and the rooms which we use, so I went to the Head of Department because I would need her OK on the changes. I got about two minutes into telling her my ideas when she interrupted me saying she had made all the arrangements for the next academic year for the timetables, rooms, etc. She suggested that I concentrate on recruiting up to target for the next year and that was it, end of meeting.
>
> (interview transcript)

Another account highlights managerial control of the workload as an issue:

> My line manager said he wanted a 'word' with me about my timetable, it turns out that one of my colleagues has gone off sick long term, we will not be getting a replacement any time soon, so I have been told I will have to take on some of the teaching, the rest will be shared by colleagues. I pointed out to him that I was already working over the agreed hours, but that made no difference, the trainees are there, they need to be taught . . . I'm running to stand still at the moment, there is not much time for reflection.
>
> (interview transcript)

Suter noted that this managerialism can have an effect on relationships with colleagues and the opportunities for collaborative reflective practice. In an interview a FE teacher stated:

We have a grumble and sometimes a bit of a laugh about our teaching, but no one would own up to having a problem with a group or a subject they are teaching . . . I think if you did it would be seen as a bit of a weakness, you couldn't handle the work . . . if a course team is not prepared to be open with each other, that there are problems, you are not going to find solutions, but staff do not like the idea of any of their problems with teaching finding their way onto an appraisal form, so it's heads down and get on with it.

Suter did however find that though the discourse of managerialism was pervasive, it did not entirely determine the relationships between teachers and their managers and colleagues. He quotes one student teacher as saying:

. . . recently I was looking at some of the handbooks and worksheets (for a counselling course) and I thought the examples given did not show the experience of black people, particularly women, you know, the pressures they are under. I wrote down some of my thoughts and discussed them with one of (course) team. She suggested I took it to the weekly team meeting for discussion. We discussed the issues and we agreed there should be changes next year . . . you feel you can discuss things [with her manager], you feel your ideas are listened to . . . that you can change things, to improve the courses.

This example seems to suggest that though there might be constraints placed on the process of reflective practice it is possible that the relationships with colleagues and managers can be an enabling one.

The final concern about the culture of the LLS and reflective practice is that there is a danger that reflection on practice might be 'co-opted' by managerialism. For instance this can happen where the teacher is required to reflect on their own 'performance' as part of an appraisal process, or even after each teaching session. There are two interrelated problems with this absorption of reflection on practice into a quality assurance/improvement system. First there may be a perception among teachers that this is an invitation to 'confess' shortcomings in professional practice and second that teachers will be circumspect in what they record in their reflections, knowing that they will be read by their managers. The dangers here are obvious. A requirement by management for their staff to record their reflections on practice could result in the strategic compliance stated as an issue above. This would result in an impoverished reflection, doing the minimum to satisfy requirements. A greater problem however is that teachers would not be open about the issues facing them in their professional practice, an openness which is an important part of effective reflection on practice.

Conclusion

The title of this chapter is 'Problems and Limitations'. There are indeed concerns with the engagement with reflective practice and there are the constraints of the culture of the LLS and individual organizations on effective reflection. They are not however reasons for abandoning reflection on learning and professional practice. It may be that teacher educators need to emphasize more the benefits of reflection to their student teachers. The management of individual education and training providers in the LLS might consider the benefits to the learners and the organization of having teachers engage in a reflective practice independent of quality assurance systems. A way forward has been shown by the Institute for Learning (IfL 2008) that gives its members the opportunity to reflect on their own learning and practice and identify their own professional development needs.

Practical activity

This is an extract from a student teacher's written reflections on her teaching:

> The class started at 9.00 am. The learners started to arrive as usual at ten past, and I managed to make a start at 9.20. As the topic for the morning was researching for project work, I got the learners to log on to the college VLP (virtual learning platform). There were the usual moans from some of the learners that they could not 'get the computer to work'. I sorted this out in most cases and got some of them to double up on a PC where necessary. I was then able to help individual learners with their work. Once again I had to remind about half of them of what the project was about and what was expected of them. After that it was the usual struggle to keep all the learners working steadily on the research. Some of them were looking on sites which had little to do with the project. Most of the learners did however manage to collect some useful information which they could use in their project.
>
> We had a break at 10.30 and resumed at 10.45. It took some time to get everybody back on track and we had about 45 minutes of productive work before the learners started to get restless. The last half hour was the usual cajoling to finish the work. The class ended at 12.00.

- Why might the way this teacher is reflecting on her practice prevent her from improving her practice?
- What questions might this teacher ask herself about this session to begin to improve the learner experience?

9

Some theoretical perspectives

In this chapter we will outline the work of those thinkers and writers who can be said to have had an influence on the development of reflective practice and use of professional judgement. Most of them did not write about teaching *per se*, nonetheless each of them had something to say about the importance of individuals developing the ability to reflect upon their attitudes and actions to enable them to meet the challenges they face in the conduct of their affairs. In discussing their work, two themes will be explored. The first is that the world is a complex place, and that often there is not an 'off the peg' decision to make or solution to be found. If this view of the world is accepted, it follows that is important for individuals to develop 'judgement' to be able to make decisions and find solutions. The second theme is that if individuals are to make effective decisions and to find solutions that work, they need the *freedom* to do so. We start with a short consideration of the 'ethics' of Aristotle, in particular the knowledge and judgement he felt was necessary to develop for individuals to live the 'good life'. Then we move on to discuss the work of arguably the most influential of modern thinkers on education, Dewey, that can be seen as a critique of a 'technicist' view of the world. This is followed by a discussion of the work of a more recent theorist who could be said to be influenced by Dewey – Kolb and his theory of experiential learning. We then turn to two theorists in the European hermeneutic tradition, Gadamer and Habermas, who in different ways may be said to support Dewey's critique of the technical-rational. Gadamer's argument for an interpretative approach to enquiry will be outlined, followed by a consideration of Habermas's on the need for critical reflection. The chapter ends with a consideration of the work of a writer very much influenced by Habermas's work – Carr. We look at his writing on developing critical reflection in teachers, which might inform a professional practice free of technical–rationalist influence.

Aristotle

We start with Aristotle, not merely because he precedes chronologically the other writers by about two thousand years, but because his writings have had such an influence on epistemology and moral philosophy. Though born in Macedonia, as a young man Aristotle moved to Athens and soon joined the intellectual circle of the city. Later in life he set up his own school in Athens, the Lyceum, where he studied and taught a wide range of human knowledge including mathematics, physical sciences, history, politics and ethics. The *Nicomachean Ethics* were written or rather compiled at this time. They were a series of lecture notes rather than what we would regard as a 'book', and were delivered to students and perhaps updated from time to time. In the *Nicomachean Ethics* (1955) (the *Ethics* from here on) Aristotle is concerned with exploring what the individual had to do and be to live the 'good life', and by extension to be a 'good man'. It should be mentioned here that Aristotle is of course writing at a time when those expected to live the good life formed a fairly narrow stratum of society made up of male citizens of the ancient Greek city.

An important aspect of the good life for Aristotle was the gaining and use of knowledge. Philosophers at this time distinguished knowledge into three areas: *techne* or 'craft knowledge', that is knowing how to make something, e.g. weaving cloth; *episteme* or 'theoretical knowledge', for example mathematical theorems; and the development of 'practical wisdom', *phronesis*. According to Aristotle, all three areas were important to society; the craft of the weaver was needed to clothe the population and theoretical knowledge helped to categorize and explain the world. *Phronesis* is that knowledge necessary for the individual to make the right decisions in life. In book six of the *Ethics*, Aristotle distinguishes it from the other two kinds of knowledge. It is the knowledge necessary to make the 'right' decision conducive to living the good life; thus right in this sense means not just finding a solution that 'works' but one that is in keeping with the individual living a 'virtuous life'. This ability to make the right decision allows the individual to cope with the uncertainties and variability of life, to deal with practical situations, hence one translation of *phronesis* is 'practical wisdom'. Korthagen (2001) draws directly upon Aristotle to argue for a development of practical wisdom in teachers. He argues that they are faced with situations in their professional practice where it is not always possible act according to a particular theory (*episteme*). Korthegen argues that theory can only act as a guide to the teacher, and the ability to make the right decision is based on 'assessing situations, judging, choosing courses of action and being confronted by their consequences' (2001: 27). How is this practical wisdom to be developed? Aristotle spoke of 'contemplation', where the individual reviews their own knowledge and thinks *rationally* about the best course of action to take based on their prior knowledge and experience. We might term this contemplation as reflection. Reflecting on learning and practice, the teacher considers the right course of action to take in their professional situation. This action might be *informed* by principle or theory but is not wholly *determined* by it. Aristotle stated in the *Ethics* that to allow decisions to be dictated by general principles was like the architect who tries to use a straight ruler on a fluted column; it does not allow for the complexities of the actual situations individuals find themselves in. This idea of the development of practical wisdom, informed by theory or principle but based firmly on the individual's rational thought or 'contemplation', we will see is an important influence on the modern writing on professional knowledge and practice.

Dewey

John Dewey is arguably the most influential educationalist of modern times, indeed his work appears in several chapters of this book. One of the reasons for this influence was the breadth of his thought and his writing, which included not only education, but also politics, social and moral philosophy. Dewey had a long life (1859–1952) that included the American Civil War, the First World War and the Second World War and he lived long enough to experience the Cold War with Soviet Russia. The context of his work however was not the span of time itself, but what happened in that time. There were massive social and economic changes in the United States of America during Dewey's life. A largely agricultural society changed into the largest industrial economy in the world. Mass immigration from the late nineteenth century onwards changed the country both socially and economically. Millions of people arrived in the growing cities to find homes and work in the large factories. These changes form the background to Dewey's work and a recurrent theme, how are we to make this society *work*?

Dewey was very much concerned with building a fair, democratic society where there should be the widest possible participation in decision making (1916). He argued that in a rapidly changing society the citizens could not rely on 'habit' (which includes social customs) to solve the problems and meet the new challenges change brings about. It is important to note for our purposes that Dewey was also developing his ideas in opposition to those we would now call the 'behaviourists', for instance the work of Taylor and his organization of work (1980) where both the means and ends of a task are identified and both are imposed on the individual. Dewey argued instead for what he called 'reflective intelligence', a fluidity of thought unhampered by 'habit'. He argued that this reflective intelligence should be nurtured through education, where rote learning of 'facts' would be replaced with a 'problem solving' approach, where children and young people would be encouraged to discuss, participate and suggest solutions to problems. It is this problem solving process which is described in Dewey's model in Chapter 3.

What are the implications of Dewey's work for reflective practice? First that we should not rely on what we have done in the past to 'to work': in a changing situation it might not. second it is unlikely that there is one 'right way' to do something, what might work in one setting might not work in another, therefore we as teachers have to be adaptable and use our reflective intelligence to find something which does work. Crucially individuals need to have the freedom to participate in problem solving and decision making; imposing methods of work on teachers hampers them in finding ways to teach and enable learning *in their situation*. It is not difficult to see why Dewey has had such an influence on reflective practice and learning.

Kolb

Kolb was among a number of writers who, while acknowledging the influence of Dewey, developed their own models and theories of education and training. Broadly these models and theories can be grouped under the heading 'Experiential learning'. Boud's model described in Chapter 3 is an example. Kolb (1984) drew on Dewey's argument that learning should be relevant to the learner, that the dichotomy between 'theory' and 'practice' was a false one, and that a way needed to be found to resolve this dichotomy. Influenced also by Dewey's ideas on 'reflective intelligence' Kolb conceived of learning as being cyclical (see Figure 9.1).

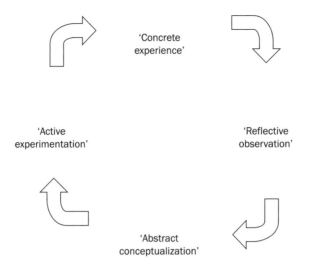

Figure 9.1 Kolb's learning cycle

'Concrete experience' is the engagement of the practice of what is being learned. In the case of the student teacher in the LLS this is of course the professional practice of teaching and enabling the learning of others. The student teacher engages in some activity with their learners: whole group teaching, enabling small group work or tutoring individual learners, for example. This experience becomes the learning material for the next stage.

The 'Reflective observation' stage is where the experience starts to be turned into learning. Kolb argued that this is where the skills of the tutor are really needed, to help 'facilitate' the learning of the learner. The tutor's task is to help the learner reflect on the learning by a process of questioning. Among these questions might be 'what happened'?, 'how did it happen'? and 'why did it happen'? Let us take for example Sarah, a student teacher who is attempting to develop her question and answer technique in the classroom. At the 'concrete experience' stage Sarah has been practising those techniques with her learners. The tutor then helps her reflect on that experience, identifying what went well, what did not go so well, and crucially *why*. Thus Sarah might reflect on why some of the responses from her learners were very short, or why some of the learners gave a hostile response to her questioning. The tutor's task is to help Sarah identify some principles of sound question and answer technique through this reflective process.

At the completion of the 'Reflective observation' stage, some general principles of what is being learned are starting to be identified, and thus we move to the 'Abstract conceptualization' point on the cycle. This is the stage where the dichotomy between theory and practice is resolved. General principles discovered with the tutor's help at the reflective observation stage can be related to the theory. If we take Sarah's example, she can relate what she experienced to the 'theory' of question and answer technique. Thus Sarah experiences and learns that a teacher should avoid the use of 'closed questions' where possible, as it limits the learner's response to 'yes' or 'no'.

The next stage of the learning cycle Kolb labelled 'active experimentation'. This is where an individual readies themselves for the next 'concrete experience' by planning to integrate the general principles learned into practice. Here Sarah might look at her planning of learning for her learners and frame some questions in the light of what she has learned about question and answer technique.

We then return to 'concrete experience', where hopefully there is an integration of practice with the theory or general principles.

Kolb's learning cycle has had a considerable influence because it has identified a way that can integrate theory and practice in learning, without making learning too abstract by ignoring practice, but also acknowledging that practice should be informed by theory and general principles.

We now turn to consider two thinkers who, while having had a considerable influence on ideas of reflection on practice and related practitioner inquiry come from a different, European tradition, that of *hermeneutics*. This is the tradition of 'interpretative' science, that any study of the 'human' or 'social' needs to take into account the understandings and interpretations of individuals, crucially in their historical and social contexts, and that seeking the 'objectivity' of the natural sciences is not only mistaken, but can actually be harmful (Bernstein 1983).

Hans-Georg Gadamer and Jurgen Habermas both worked in this hermeneutic tradition, but reached quite different conclusions, which will become clear in the following discussion of their writing.

Gadamer

In his seminal work, *Truth and Method* (1980), Gadamer states the argument for an interpretative approach to inquiry. He argues that 'objectivist' inquiry like that in the natural sciences is not appropriate in those situations where human judgement is key. Gadamer noted that all humans are born into a particular historical period and a certain culture; that none of us can somehow stand outside our history and culture. Thus our attitudes, wants and tastes will be influenced if not determined by the time and place where we were born, raised and live. The logic of this argument that no-one can take a 'God's-eye' view of human thought and action, because an individual is always part of culture, of history. According to Gadamer we are always part of some 'tradition', a way of doing things which provides a framework for how we see the world. Gadamer called this way of seeing a 'prejudice', a word which for us (in our time and place!) has very negative connotations; for him it meant that inevitably we are going to see things in a certain way because of our history and culture. This does not mean that we cannot engage in inquiry, but that the process will be interpretative, a seeking to understand, while acknowledging our own 'prejudices'.

What are the implications of Gadamer's work for reflective practice and other forms of inquiry such as action research? Gadamer drew on Aristotle to argue for the importance of 'practical wisdom', the use of professional judgement. He felt that modern industrial society relied too heavily on technical 'experts'. Elliott (1991) has developed this argument in support of teachers engaging in inquiry in their own professional situation, and not relying on outside 'experts' to instruct them on their professional practice and its development. A second important implication is that none of us can be 'objective' in the traditional scientific sense. What Gadamer argues for is an 'openness' to other ways of seeing and doing things, not to agonize over our 'prejudices' but accept that they are there and be prepared to challenge them if need be. A final point is that 'tradition' meant something positive to Gadamer; he saw it as something which helps guide thought and action, helping individuals to make judgements. Habermas argues that we should challenge tradition, to *emancipate* ourselves from its influence.

Habermas

Jurgen Habermas is alongside Dewey as the thinker who has arguably had the most influence on the theory underpinning reflective practice (Young 1989). Habermas shared some of the concerns of Dewey, defending and promulgating 'Enlightenment' values. The Enlightment was the period in the eighteenth century when much of what we would consider modern thought was established. Advances in science started to explain the natural world in terms other than religion and superstition. Technological advances in machinery and transport helped build industrial economies and meant that large populations (in certain parts of the world at least) could be fed and clothed. Significantly for both Habermas and Dewey the Enlightment was also a time when thinkers and writers were challenging the old social order based on privilege and arguing for a democratic society where the citizens would have a voice in how society was to be run. While both Dewey and Habermas can be said to defend Enlightenment values, Habermas felt that the promise of the Enlightenment – a truly democratic society – had not been fulfilled (Habermas 1984). He felt that this progress had been stalled by the imposition of hierarchies and a 'technical–rationalism' in late capitalist society (1987). He sees this not as a rationality that frees people, making society more democratic, but rather limits freedom and debate. For Habermas this 'means–end' rationalism treats the end as unproblematic, the issue being merely the most efficient and effective way of reaching those ends.

Habermas drew a distinction between two forms of human action (1984). The first is that orientated towards success. This is strategic and instrumental action. The second form of action – communicative action – is based not on calculations of individual success, but where individuals seek to reach an understanding. It is clear from his earlier work (1972) that Habermas is not discounting the need for 'instrumental action' (making sure good and services are produced and managed efficiently and effectively); he makes clear that such action and related technical knowledge is necessary for a modern society, but it is not sufficient for a democratic society to flourish.

Habermas sees in 'communicative action' the possibility of building a consensus to help build a truly democratic society. Habermas's reasoning is that reaching understanding is what human beings are striving to do when they speak to each other. He sees understanding as involving a listener's acceptance of a 'validity claim' made by the speaker. The speaker and listener will seek to communicate in a rational way in everyday discourse. Habermas argues that in late capitalist society this discourse is limited, 'systematically distorted' because of the power of technical rationality, but that in an 'Ideal Speech Situation' (ISS) individuals could seek to reach understanding without constraints being placed on communication. Young (1989), in drawing upon Habermas's work on the ISS, argues: 'It is in the facts of human speech that the possibility of freedom and respect for each human being's potential contribution to the species rests' (1989: 22). In an ISS the 'ends' as well the 'means' of action would be the subject of discourse, where goals of human action are no longer taken for granted, but become a subject for discourse. An example might be the goal of economic growth, which is often taken for granted as being a 'good thing' and the debate is more often than not about the means of achieving it – the 'technical' arguments of whether tax cuts work etc.

It is this questioning of 'means–end' rationalism advocated by Habermas that influenced what has become known as 'critical reflective practice'. Hillier (2002: 25) argues for it in this way:

> We can become positive in our search for new understandings of practice and more ways to deal with the challenges that confront us continually. We take control over our professional practice, acknowledging we cannot transform everything, but aware we can identify the spheres we can.

This chimes with a 'stakeholder' view of education and training (Avis 2005) where teachers, alongside the government, government agencies, managers, employers, community groups, parents and of course learners themselves would have a say in the formulation of policy and the conduct of education and training. In this view teachers would have a 'voice', the chance to have views heard by other stakeholders in education and training. These views would be based on the process of critical reflective practice undertaken by the practitioners on not just the technical aspects of teaching and learning, but also on policy and the organization of education and training, both at a local and national level. This it might be argued would counter the 'means–end' technical rationalism which assumes that all the goals of education and training are already agreed and therefore beyond debate.

Carr

Wilfred Carr is the educationalist who has perhaps gone the farthest in integrating Habermas's thought into a critical theory on education. Carr (1995) has advocated the adoption of what he calls an 'education science', distinguished from the sciences such as psychology, which he argued that while having a powerful influence on education are not always relevant to the *practice* of teaching and enabling learning (Carr and Kemmis 1986). In his book *For Education: Towards Critical Educational Inquiry* (1995) Carr sets out the case for a 'critical social science', drawing on Habermas's critical theory. The starting point for Carr's critical inquiry is the 'knowledge interests' identified by Habermas (1972), which in turn are in part based on Aristotle's modes of reasoning described earlier in this chapter. Developing Aristotle's modes, Habermas stated that different forms of knowledge did not just employ different modes of reasoning, but that they also served different interests. He argued that some knowledge served a *technical* interest, concerned as we have seen in the discussion of Habermas's work above with the 'material' world to serve human needs and wants; the science of chemistry is an example of this. Drawing once more on Aristotle's modes of reasoning, Habermas named the second 'knowledge–interest' the *practical*.

The sense of practical here is that knowledge which is concerned with guiding and informing, by interpreting the world so that informed choices might be made by society, history, sociology and psychology are examples of these social sciences. Habermas added to these modes another knowledge-interest – the *emancipatory*, concerned with issues of justice and freedom as the term suggests. This is the basis for a 'critical social science' which both offers a critique of how society (including education) is organized and governed, but also organizes action to make social and political changes. This emancipatory knowledge-interest for Carr becomes a 'critical educational science'. This critical approach Carr sets against the others that teachers might take towards reflection on teaching and learning. The first he calls a 'common-sense' approach; this entails identifying 'best practice' in teaching and learning, but without regard to any theory or other body of published work. Thus this for Carr is 'to engage in a educational practice . . . to think and act in conformity with the concepts, knowledge and skills of a given tradition (1995: 47).

The second approach Carr identified was that of 'applied science'. In this approach teaching and learning are subject to scientific methods of investigation. Here good practice is identified through the rigorous use of those methods, usually by researchers from outside the professional setting where the research is taking place. Third there is the 'practical' approach, which is perhaps the closest to Aristotle's 'practical wisdom'. Teaching and learning is seen as a complex, indeterminate form of human action calling for the use of reflection and of professional judgement. Unlike the applied science approach, any theory developed through investigating teaching and learning cannot provide rigorous scientific knowledge, but rather guidance for professional judgment of what *might* be done in a particular situation. The fourth 'critical' approach goes beyond this interpretative Gadamerian route to investigating teaching and learning. Carr argues that the 'practical' concern with the subjective understandings of teachers and the 'applied science' concern with objective explanation can be reconciled in the 'critical' approach. Carr states that the aim of critical educational inquiry is to 'increase the rational autonomy of practitioners' (1995: 50). To do this teachers should undertake 'critical self reflection' to explore both their own beliefs and practices and the institutional and social context within which those beliefs and practices emerge.

Conclusion

A reading of these theorists demonstrates that is possible to challenge the view of the professional practice of teaching as being reducible to a list of prescriptions to be followed, that if correctly done will produce the 'right' result. Though there might be some differences in perspectives, Gadamer and Habermas and the writers who draw on them agree that a 'technical' view of the world is too prescriptive and does not deal effectively with the complexities and challenges of that world. Writers such as Carr remind us that education and training are part of that world, and to grasp the complexities and deal with the challenges teachers should be encouraged to *critically* reflect on their learning and practice.

10
Conclusion

In this chapter we summarize the reasons for teachers and lecturers to engage in reflection on practice and learning and some of the ways that this might be done as espoused throughout this book. We sat down and reflected upon our experiences as subject teachers and teacher educators, and on what we had written for this book, and the following points are a result of those reflections. In writing them we wish to avoid glib exhortations to reflect and we acknowledge that the process is not always an easy one, but at the same time we want to highlight the benefits of that engagement.

We start with the point that reflecting on learning and practice is a requirement made of both student teachers and trained teachers in the LLS. Student teachers will almost without exception be required by their teacher education tutors to reflect on teaching and learning. As we have remarked in Chapter 7, as part of their continuing professional development experienced and trained teachers in the LLS are required by their professional body, the IfL, to reflect on their practice and in particular their development needs. We have noted in Chapter 8 that making reflection a requirement can present problems but it is possible to see these requirements in a positive light. It can be seen as an acknowledgement that first it is not possible to be too prescriptive about teaching and that teachers should be encouraged to develop their own professional judgement. Second it is an opportunity for teachers to take some control over their own professional development and not leave it to chance, or worse to have that development imposed upon them.

If reflection on learning and practice were not a compulsory requirement, what then would be the reasons for reflecting? As authors we have considered the number of times our own professional practice has been observed and appraised and in both cases it amounted to an average of one appraisal meeting and one teaching observation per year. Considering the amount of teaching undertaken by us this amounts to a tiny percentage of our time in this professional situation. We acknowledge that teaching situations vary widely in the LLS but nevertheless the majority of teachers find themselves solely responsible for a group of learners for much of the time. In this situation the person best placed to consider improvements and changes in professional practice is the teacher through a process of reflection on practice.

However reflection will not be effective unless it is *systematic*. Most teachers give some thought to their professional practice: the successes, the failures and how things might be improved. It is sustained, planned reflection that will result in the desired changes. In Chapter 2 we noted that the process of reflection does not have to be complex or unduly technical. The basic model of reflection can be used right away by the novice teacher to give consideration to the practice of teaching. Using such a model allows the less experienced teacher to give due regard to the 'nuts and bolts' of their practice, for example the selection of teaching and learning strategies and classroom management.

An important aspect of systematic reflection is the integration of theory and practice. Applying theory without regard to the actual situation in which teaching and learning is taking place does not 'work'. For example one of us observed a student teacher trying inappropriately to use behaviourist principles of learning in a drama class and when asked about this in the feedback session at the end of the observation the student remarked that he thought he should use 'some theory'. Conversely the practice of teaching which is not informed by theory, or at least published 'good practice', is impoverished. The process of reflection on learning and practice enables the teacher to integrate theory or other published knowledge into professional practice in a pragmatic way, with a due regard for what 'works'.

The teacher may work in isolation from colleagues for much of the time. The process of reflection however can include the consideration of others' perspectives in the professional situation. In Chapter 5 we discussed how feedback and support from teacher education tutors and mentors can be drawn upon to help improve and develop professional practice. An important point to remember here is that once the teacher has received advice or feedback from a tutor or mentor it is incumbent upon them to reflect on how what has been suggested can actually be integrated into professional practice. In Chapter 3 we noted that Brookfield's model of reflection includes 'critical lenses', not only of the teacher and colleagues but also of the learners, who after all are at the receiving end of the teaching!

There are times when the teacher is seeking not only to change and improve their practice, but wishes to address wider issues, perhaps course organization or setting up an effective tutorial system. In this situation the teacher will need to collaborate with colleagues to bring change and improvement about. Chapter 4 gives examples of how this might be done in an effective way to make improvements and changes which work in a particular professional situation.

In Chapter 6 we discussed how the engagement in reflective practice might be extended into action research, a form of inquiry where teachers identify the issues relevant to them in their own situation and seek to find solutions which work for them, rather than taking them 'off the peg' from consultants, etc. Action research is a logical extension of reflection on practice because there is a reflective cycle at the heart of the action research model.

In our concern to avoid mere exhortations to reflect on practice and learning we acknowledge that there can be problems in engaging in reflection and indeed limitations to its use. There is a danger that if a requirement to reflect on practice and learning is *imposed* on teachers it will result in strategic compliance, i.e. a 'going through the motions' approach to reflection. We believe that this can be avoided if both student teachers and experienced practitioners are given the time and opportunity to engage in reflection which makes a real difference to the professional practice of teaching and enabling learning. This brings us on to the issue of organizational culture and reflection. In Chapter 7 we noted that some cultures are more conducive to the process of reflection than others. Though a full discussion of managerial cultures in the LLS is beyond the scope of this book it is only fair to say that there might be some situations where the chances to effect changes and improvements to professional practice might be limited.

We want to finish the book on a cautionary note. Our varied experiences of teaching have convinced us of the centrality of the process of reflection on learning and practice. It does not have to be an overly technical process: novice teachers can start to reflect from day one as we have shown in this book. Reflection on learning and practice is an effective way of integrating theory or 'published knowledge' with practice, so that theory can *inform* practice. It helps you as the teacher to avoid relying on prescriptions on what *should* work in teaching and learning and discover what actually *does* work. In taking this pragmatic view, teachers can take decisions on those elements of their professional practice in their control and understand (and perhaps critique) those elements that influence their professional practice.

References

Ainley, P. and Bailey, B. (1997) *The Business of Learning: Staff and Student Experiences of Further Education in the 1990s*. London: Cassell.

Aristotle (1955) *The Nichomachean Ethics* (trans. J. Thomson). London: Penguin.

Armitage, A. (2007) *Teaching and Training in Post-compulsory Education*, 3rd edn. Maidenhead: Open University Press.

Avis, J. (1999) Rethinking trust in a performative culture: the case of education, *Journal of Education Policy*, 18(3): 245–64.

Avis, J. (1999) Shifting identity – new conditions and the transformation of practice: teaching within post-compulsory education, *Journal of Vocational Education and Training*, 51(2): 245–64.

Avis, J. (2003) Rethinking trust in a performative culture, *Journal of Education Policy*, 18(3): 315–22.

Avis, J. (2005) Beyond performativity: reflections on activist professionalism and the labour process, *Journal of Education Policy*, 20(2): 209–22.

Avis, J., Bathmaker, A. M. and Parson, J. (2001) Reflections from a time log diary: towards an analysis of the labour process within further education, *Journal of Education and Training*, 53(1): 61–80.

Avis, J., Fisher, R. and Thompson, R. (eds) (2010) *Teaching in Lifelong Learning: A Guide to Theory and Practice*. Maidenhead: Open University Press.

Ball, S.J. (2003) The teacher's soul and the terrors of performativity, *Journal of Education Policy*, 18(2): 215–28.

Bernstein, B. (1983) *Beyond Objectivism and Relativism: Science, Hermeneutics and Praxis*. Oxford: Basil Blackwell.

Boud, D., Keogh, R. and Walker, D. (1985) *Reflection: Turning Reflection into Learning*. London: Kogan Page.

Brookfield, S. (1995) *Becoming a Critically Reflective Teacher*. San Francisco, CA: Jossey Bass.

Brown, P., Lauder, H. and Ashton, D. (2008) *Education, Globalisation and the Knowledge Economy*, TLRP commentary. London: University of London.

Burton, S., Fisher, R., Lord, D. and Webb, K. (2010) Subject specialist pedagogy, in J. Avis, R. Fisher and R. Thompson (eds) *Teaching in Lifelong Learning*. Maidenhead: McGraw-Hill.

Carr, W. (1995) *For Education: Towards Critical Educational Inquiry*. Buckingham: Open University Press.

Carr, W. and Kemmis, S. (1986) *Education, Knowledge and Action Research*. Lewes: Falmer Press.

Coffield, F. (2008) *Just Suppose Teaching and Learning Became the First Priority*. London: Learning and Skills Network.

Cowan, J. (1998) *On Becoming an Innovative University Teacher*. Buckingham: SRHE and Open University Press.

Dewey, J. (1916) *Democracy and Education*. New York: Macmillan.

Dewey, J. (1933) *How We Think*. Chicago: Regnary.

DIUS (2008) *Further Education Colleges – Models for Success*. London: Department for Innovation, Universities and Skills.

Duckett, I. and Tatarkowsky, M. (2005) *Practical Strategies for Learning and Teaching on Vocational Programmes*. London: LSDA.

Ebbutt, D. (1985) *Educational Action Research: Some General Concerns and Specific Quibbles*, in R. Burgess (ed.) *Issues in Educational Research*. Lewes: Falmer Press.

Elliott, J. (1991) *Action Research for Educational Change*. Buckingham: Open University Press.

Feuerstein, R., Klein, P.S. and Tannenbaum, A.J. (1994) *Mediated Learning Experience (MLE): Theoretical, Psychosocial and Learning Implications*. London: Freund Publishing.

Foster, A. (2005) *Realising the Potential: A Review of the Future Role of Further Education Colleges*. Annesley: DfES.

Furlong, J. (2003) *Intuition and the Crisis in Teacher Professionalism*, in T. Atkinson and G. Claxton (2003) *The Intuitive Practitioner*. Buckingham: Open University Press.

Gadamer, H.-G. (1980) *Truth and Method*, (trans. G.Bardey and J.Cummings). New York: Seabury Press.

Gleeson, D., Davies, J. and Wheeler, E. (2005) On the making and taking of professionalism in the further education workplace, *British Journal of Sociology of Education*, 26(3): 445–60.

Goldhill, R. (2009) Reflective practice and distance learning: problems and potentials for probation training, *Reflective Practice*, 11(1): 57–70.

Habermas, J. (1972) *Knowledge and Human Interests* (trans. J. Shapiro). London: Heinemann.

Habermas, J. (1984) *The Theory of Communicative Action, Vol. 1: Reason and the Rationalization of Society* (trans. T. McCarthy). Boston, MA: Beacon Press.

Habermas, J. (1987) *The Theory of Communicative Action, Vol. 2: A Critique of Functionalist Reason* (trans. T. McCarthy). Boston, MA: Beacon Press.

Hanks, P. (ed.) (1979) *Collins English Dictionary*. London: Collins.

Hillier, Y. (2002) *Reflective Teaching in Further and Adult Education*. London: Continuum.

Hobbs, V. (2007) Faking it or hating it: can reflective practice be forced? *Reflective Practice*, 8(3): 405–17.

Hodkinson, P. (1998) Technicism, teachers and teacher quality in vocational education and training, *Journal of Vocational Education and Training*, 50(2): 193–224.

Hodkinson, P. and James, D. (2003) Introduction of transforming learning cultures in further education, *Journal of Education and Training*, 55(4): 389–406.

Hopkins, D. (2002) *A Teacher's Guide to Classroom Research*, 3rd edn. Buckingham: Open University Press.

Husu, J., Patrikainen, S. and Toom, A. (2008) Guided reflection as a means to demonstrate and develop teachers' reflective competencies, *Reflective Practice*, 9(1): 37–51.

IfL (Institute for Learning) (2008) *Licence to Practice: Professional Formation*. London: IfL.

James, D. and Biesta, G. (eds) (2007) *Improving Learning Cultures in Further Education*. London: Routledge.

Jarvis, M. (2005) *The Psychology of Effective Teaching and Learning*. Cheltenham: Nelson Thornes.

Keep, E. (2006) State control of the English education and training system – playing with the biggest train set in the world, *Journal of Vocational Education and Training*, 58(1): 47–64.

Kemmis, S. and McTaggart, R. (1981) *The Action Research Planner*. Victoria: Deakin University Press.

Kolb, D.A. (1984) *Experiential Learning: Experience as the Source of Learning and Development.* Englewood Cliffs, NJ: Prentice Hall.

Korthagen, F. (2001) *Linking Practice and Theory: The Pedagogy of Realistic Teacher Education.* Mahwah, NJ: Lawrence Erlbaum Associates.

Lave, J. and Wenger, E. (1991) *Situated Learning: Legitimate Peripheral Participation.* Cambridge: Cambridge University Press.

Leitch, S. (2006) *Prosperity for All in the Global Economy: World Class Skills.* Norwich: Her Majesty's Stationery Office.

Lewin, K. (1946) Action research and minority problems, *Journal of Social Issues,* 2(4): 32–46.

LLUK (2005) *New Overarching Professional Standards for Teachers, Tutors and Trainers in the Lifelong Learning Sector.* London: Lifelong Learning UK.

McNiff, J. (1993) *Teaching as Learning: An Action Research Approach.* London: Routledge.

Maynard, T. and Furlong, J. (1995) Learning to teach and models of mentoring, in T. Kerry and A.S. Mayes (eds) (1995) *Issues in Mentoring.* London: Routledge with the Open University.

Moon, J.A. (2006) *Learning Journals: A Handbook for Reflective Practice and Professional Development.* Abingdon: Routledge.

Ofsted (2003) *The Initial Training of Further Education Teachers: A Survey,* HMI 1762. London: Office for Standards in Education.

Ofsted (2009) *Grade Criteria for the Inspection of Initial Teacher Education 2008–11.* London: Office for Standards in Education.

Orr, K. and Simmons, R.A. (2009) Dual Identities: The In-Service trainee teacher experience in the English Further Education sector. Paper presented at the *Journal of Vocational Education and Training* 8th International Conference, Worcester College, Oxford, 3–5 July.

Petty, G. (1993) *Teaching Today: A Practical Guide.* Cheltenham: Stanley Thornes.

Petty, G. (2004) *Teaching Today: A Practical Guide.* Chettenham: Nelson Thornes.

Pollard, A. (2002) *Reflective Teaching: Effective and Evidence-informed Professional Practice.* London: Continuum.

Prensky, M. (2001) Digital natives, digital immigrants, *On the Horizon* 9(5): 1–2.

Randle, K. and Brady, R. (1997) Managerialism and professionalism in the Cinderella service, *Journal of Vocational Education and Training,* 49(1): 52–66.

Reynolds, B. and Suter, M. (2010) *Reflective Practice,* in J. Avis, R. Fisher and R. Thompson (eds) (2010) *Teaching in Lifelong Learning: A Guide To Theory and Practice.* Maidenhead: Open University Press.

Ritzer, G. (1998) *The McDonaldization Thesis.* London: Sage.

Robinson, D. (2009) *CPD in Practice – How is it Valuable? A Personal Reflection.* www. cpdinstitute.org/documents (accessed 25 February 2011).

Schön, D.A. (1983) *The Reflective Practitioner: How Professionals Think in Action.* London: Temple Smith.

Schön, D.A. (1987) *Educating the Professional Practitioner: Towards a New Design For Teaching in the Professions.* San Fransisco, CA: Jossey Bass.

Shain, F. and Gleeson, D. (1999) Under New Management: changing conceptions of teacher professionalism and policy in the further education sector, *Journal of Education Policy,* 14(4):445–62.

Somekh, B. (2006) *Action Research: A Methodology for Change and Development.* Maidenhead: Open University Press.

Stenhouse, L. (1975) *An Introduction to Curriculum Research and Development.* London: Heinemann.

Suter, M. (2007) Constructing the reflective practitioner: A Critical account. Unpublished Doctorate of Education thesis, Manchester Metropolitan University.

Taylor, P.H. (1980) *An Introduction to Curriculum Studies.* Windsor: NFER.

Thompson, M. and William, D. (2007) Tight But Loose: a conceptual framework for scaling up school reforms, in F. Coffield (ed.) *Just Suppose Teaching and Learning Became the First Priority.* London: Learning and Skills Network.

Tripp, D. (1993) *Critical Incidents in Teaching: Developing Professional Judgement.* London: Routledge

Usher, R. and Edwards, R. (1994) *Postmodernism and Education.* London: Routledge.

Vygotsky, L.S. (1978) *Mind in Society: The Development of Higher Psychological Processes.* Cambridge, MA: Harvard University Press.

Williams, S. (2003) Conflict in the colleges: industrial relations in FE since incorporation, *Journal of Further and Higher Education*, 27(3): 307–15.

Wilson, A.L. (1994) To a middle ground: praxis and ideology in adult education, *International Journal of Lifelong Education*, 13(3): 187–202.

Woods, P. (1986) *Inside Schools: Ethnography in Educational Research.* London: Routledge.

Young, R. (1989) *A Critical Theory of Education: Habermas and Our Childrens' Future.* London: Harvester Wheatsheaf.

Index